A Worthy Woman

"her price is far above rubies"

Proverbs 31.10–31

Darlene Craig

DEWARD
PUBLISHING COMPANY

A Worthy Woman (revised)
© 2011 by DeWard Publishing Company, Ltd.
P.O. Box 6259, Chillicothe, Ohio 45601
800.300.9778
www.deward.com

Cover design by Jonathan Hardin.

Any emphasis in Bible quotations is added.

Printed in the United States of America.

ISBN: 978-1-936341-19-1

This labor of love is dedicated with my love to the "distaff," or feminine side of our family, in the order they came into our family beginning with our daughter, Melisa, Susan, Anneliese, Linda, Paige, Olivia, Madeline, Hope, Faith, Gracie, Emma, Jessica, and Charlotte.

THANK YOU

With loving thanks to my beloved, ever loving husband Al who is ever kind, ever encouraging, and ever willing to solve countless computer complications for typewriter loyal, unmechanical me.

Thank you to my dear sister in Christ, Marisa Walker, for taking time from her young family and other responsibilities to retype my messy manuscript into the computer.

Most of all, I am prayerfully thankful to "the God and Father of our Lord Jesus Christ" who strengthened me to complete this study, with a prayer in my heart that it will be a worthwhile work of encouragement to others.

INTRODUCTION

The First Lady moves about the city. Early morning duties done or delegated, her concern for others propels the projects she chooses for the day. Buoyed by her husband's confidence in her, she pursues plans of interest to both. The strength, integrity, and ability she brings to this important position furthers her effectiveness. Her words and actions reflect her values, and the values of those she represents, and help her help others.

Her noble attitude and perception feed her enthusiasm, and she is confident at the prospects for the future. The encouragement she receives from those close to her and others who feel her influence, refreshes. Her strength is renewed as she thinks of the focus of her life, and the rewards to come.

The First Lady of our land? No. The First Lady of Proverbs 31. Many First Ladies of our country have been women of honor, intelligence, talent, loyalty, faith, and compassion. Eager attitudes have ensured their many admirable qualities produced worthwhile accomplishments, and deserved praise. The same is true of the First Lady of Proverbs 31, a worthy woman, and the same is true of worthy women today.

Still, today's woman continues to be bombarded with the belief that her position as wife and mother isn't honored, limits her influence, and wastes her intelligence, talents, and education. This isn't the picture the Proverbs 31 woman presents, and it isn't the true picture of the wife and mother of today.

This study of Proverbs 31 begins with verse 10, since many

scholars think verses 1–9 a separate section, with verse 10 beginning a new section describing "a worthy woman…." Verse 10 tells you she is a worthy woman. The next 21 verses show you.

A detailed study erases the "why tries?" that a quick read-through can bring on. Was this passage designed to discourage? Rather, it encourages real women today to embrace the joyful attitude and purposeful actions of this ideal woman. And even she didn't do it all at the same time. Many of her activities were seasonal. Others were during different seasons of her life, but her inner strength, her devotion, her joy, her industry, her care for others, are for every season, every circumstance, and every godly woman.

Proverbs 31.10–31 excels as a guidebook to excellence. Most things of worth take guidance and know-how. Certainly our womanhood. To it we bring various strengths and weaknesses. We each have unique personalities and experiences that challenge, or bring richness to our relationships.

Women differ in the areas that are easy or difficult. This is true of anything we attempt. For example in sewing, one woman grits her teeth and tortures the material as she cuts it. Another has no problem there but weeps as she tries to master the machine. I find it surprising that some like to put in zippers.

Reactions vary in all areas of home life. Some feel squelched by their lifestyle. The daily domestic routine is a nightmare to many. To others, the thought of raising children is hair-raising. Some think the husband-wife relationship almost impossible and claim the area of subjection as their personal Gethsemane. Some whiz through all these, face down other difficulties, and still question their worth.

In this passage of scripture, the inspired writer uses distinctive word pictures that help you use the life of the "far above rubies" woman to realize your value and enrich your life and the lives of others. It motivates you to joyfully pursue a God-centered, hope filled life that maximizes your potential for doing good to those within your home and others within your reach.

Knowing "these things were written for our learning" (Rom

15.4), this study uses the worthy woman's example of excellence to strengthen, encourage, and equip women today, whether they are struggling to make the most out of a mess or to be good stewards of a blessed life.

WHAT TO EXPECT

Thirteen Chapters
Each chapter of *A Worthy Woman* covers one or more verses from Proverbs 31.10–31.

At The End Of Each Chapter...

• **Questions**

• **Strength Training**
Suggestions and To Do's for class discussion, or personal thought or action, to further growth in the Worthy Woman's inner quality of strength.

• **Worthy Women**
Highlights qualities of women of Old or New Testament times. Exceptions: Chaper 9 features a Worthy Man and Chapter 13 is a tribute to Worthy Women Of Today.

• **Facets**
Reflections relating to a facet of the life of the "far above rubies" woman, or just life.

CONTENTS

CHAPTER EIGHT 121

She is not afraid of the snow for her household; for all her household are clothed with scarlet. She maketh for herself carpets of tapestry; Her clothing is fine linen and purple.

Prepared... Personal Projects... Making the Most of It... Time Out for You... Her Clothing... What Shall We Wear?... Esther...Taking Time

CHAPTER NINE 131

Her husband is known in the gates, when he sitteth among the elders of the land. She maketh linen garments and selleth them, And delivereth girdles unto the merchants.

In the Gates... New Testament Elders... Worthy Men... Worthless Men... Wardrobes... Extra Activities... Ezekiel... Spiritual Oneness.

CHAPTER TEN 141

Strength and dignity are her clothing; and she laugheth at the time to come.

The Weak Woman Myth... Future Welcome Here...Tranquility with a Twinkle... Empty Nest... Reunited?... Alone... Hattie... Jochebed... Sorrow-Mysterious Magnet?

CHAPTER ELEVEN 153

She openeth her mouth with wisdom; And the law of kindness is on her tongue.

Wise Words... Slow to Speak... Foolish Words... WIWO... Laying Down the Law... Criticism KOs Kindness... Rat-a-Tat-Tongue... Your Own Business... Archery... Abigail...Euodia and Syntyche

CHAPTER TWELVE 163

She looketh well to the ways of her household, And eateth not the bread of idleness.

Teaching Technique... Heart to Heart... A Mother's Heart... Spiritual Starter Dough... Fathers Too... Choices... Pro Teen... "Big Bird"... Mary and Elizabeth... Anywhere With Jesus.

Her children rise up and call her blessed; Her husband also, and he praiseth her, saying many daughters have done worthily, But thou excellest them all. Grace is deceitful, and beauty is vain; But a woman that feareth Jehovah, she shall be praised. Give her of the fruit of her hands; and let her works praise her in the gates.

Finale of Praise... Reward Snatching... Her Husband's Praise... Is Fluff Enough?... Inner Splendor... Stand in Awe... Stolen Identity... Shared Rewards... Mixed Fruit... Velda... Full Reward... Framed in Faith... Worthy Women of Today... Extra Mile Attitude

A worthy woman who can find?
For her price is far above rubies.
The heart of her husband trusteth in her,
And he shall have no lack of gain.
She doeth him good and not evil
All the days of her life.
She seeketh wool and flax,
And worketh willingly with her hands.
She is like the merchant-ships;
She bringeth her bread from afar.
She riseth also while it is yet night,
And giveth food to her household,
And their task to her maidens.
She considereth a field, and buyeth it;
With the fruit of her hands she planteth a vineyard.
She girdeth her loins with strength,
And maketh strong her arms.
She perceiveth that her merchandise is profitable;
Her lamp goeth not out by night.
She layeth her hands to the distaff,
And her hands hold the spindle.
She stretcheth out her hand to the poor
Yea, she reacheth forth her hands to the needy.
She is not afraid of the snow for her household;
For all her household are clothed with scarlet.
She maketh for herself carpets of tapestry;
Her clothing is fine linen and purple.
Her husband is known in the gates,
When he sitteth among the elders of the land.
She maketh linen garments and selleth them,
And delivereth girdles unto the merchant.

Strength and dignity are her clothing;
And she laugheth at the time to come.
She openeth her mouth with wisdom;
And the law of kindness is on her tongue.
She looketh well to the ways of her household,
And eateth not the bread of idleness.
Her children rise up, and call her blessed;
Her husband also, and he praiseth her, saying
Many daughters have done worthily,
But thou excellest them all.
Grace is deceitful, and beauty is vain;
But a woman that feareth Jehovah, she shall be praised.
Give her of the fruit of her hands;
And let her works praise her in the gates.

Proverbs 31.10–31

ONE

A worthy woman, who can find?
For her price is far above rubies.

"I feel worthless." Beneath her blonde wig, the thin, 30ish woman blinked back tears with her false eyelashes. "I can't remember being happy a day in my life." Frustration and grief spilled over with her tears. She was "trying to quit swearing." She had given up tequila. "I drank to cope."

Now, grieving the loss of her infant to crib death, and dying of cancer, she longed for a new life in her time left on earth and the eternity to come. Later, we rejoiced with her as she was washed free of her burdens, felt new strength for her struggles, and realized her worth as a child of God.

It occurred to me as I thought about her unusually sad life that many women, even those already walking in "newness of life," feel worthless. Some feel their past is sabotaging their present. Some feel overwhelmed by present circumstances. Some feel overworked and underappreciated. Some feel lonely and unloved. Some say their worth as women is undervalued and feel little hope of reward.

Proverbs 31.10–31 raises a window shade on the life of a worthy woman and lets the light of the scripture illuminate our lives with hope, peace, and perspective.

The ABCs of It

This compact library of inspiration and information helps today's woman live a joyful, purposeful life. The passage fits the acrostic form since each of the 22 verses begins with a Hebrew letter in the order of the Hebrew alphabet. Verse 10 begins with aleph, the first letter of the Hebrew alphabet. Verse 11 begins with beth, the second letter. This order continues through the 22 verses and is the reason this well-known acrostic is sometimes called the "ABCs of the Ideal Woman."

The worthy woman is an ideal woman rather than a real woman, but as we live her everyday life through these verses she comes alive to us. As we feel their impact on our lives, she will seem more like a friend than a faraway figure.

Worthy Defined

"A *worthy* woman." A brief study of the word "worthy" reveals her character. This is important since her character affects each area and relationship in her life, just as your character, your personality, the real you, affects every area and relationship of your life.

The American Standard Version uses "worthy" in verse 10. Strong's Concordance defines "worthy" with such words as strength, substance, power, valor, and virtuous. These qualities weren't superimposed on a weak woman. They were embedded in her worthy heart.

They also fit well with the New American Standard Version, and the New American Standard Update's use of "excellent" in verse 10. Excellent includes "valor, being remarkably good—exceptional." The worthy woman was outstanding in every area portrayed in Proverbs 31.10–31. Many versions also use a form of "excellent" in verse 29. The worthy woman was the essence of excellence.

Perhaps the most familiar translation of "worthy" is "virtuous" from the King James Version and the New King James Version. "Virtuous" means "strength, moral strength, good quality, integrity or virtue." The Pulpit Commentary says: Virtuous "combines the ideas of moral goodness and bodily vigor and activity." The International Standard Bible Encyclopedia includes "strength," "force," (whether of body or mind). Then in a moral sense of worth... virtue." The worthy woman has "strength of soul."

Inner Olympics

Proverbs 31.10–31 spotlights the inner strength and integrity of this exceptional woman. She gets the gold in the inner Olympics. Though also physically strong, her high spiritual and moral standards set this praiseworthy woman apart.

God's word sets the standard. "Be ye therefore imitators of God..." (Eph 5.1). "But like as he who called you is holy, be ye yourselves also holy in all manner of living; because it is written, 'Ye shall be holy; for I am holy'" (1 Pet 1.15–16).

The worthy woman didn't turn from her focus of faith "unto idols" of that era (Lev 19.4). It takes a strong spiritual and moral backbone and vigor to keep from conforming to society's standards, whether ancient or modern, "to approve the things that are excellent" (Phil 1.10). As we sort out our lives and set our goals, let's choose the biblical standard of godliness as a goal worth striving for throughout our lifetime.

Role Model Par Excellence

The word virtuous also suggests the idea of inspiring to imitate. Though the worthy woman can have this effect, she is usually overlooked in the search for role models. Those seriously searching often look to the lives of singers and musicians, runway models, sports celebrities, heroines of novels and soap operas, TV and movie stars. Hollywood instead of His holy word. Many disappoint.

Why not look to the Bible where verses, chapters, and even books inspire with women of excellence? For example, if you read only the book of Ruth through 1 Samuel 25, you will find four such women: Ruth, Naomi, Hannah, and Abigail. Ruth held no prominent position in Bethlehem, yet her story merited an entire book in which Boaz praised her citywide example of a "worthy woman" (Ruth 3.11). Many of her qualities are the same ones the worthy woman exemplifies.

As a widow, Ruth's circumstances were different, but she too was God-fearing, strong, devoted, kind, and industrious. As Ruth gleaned in the fields, let us glean wisdom and insight from her example, and from our role model par excellence, the worthy woman of Proverbs 31.10–31. (See Worthy Woman Ruth—End of Ch.)

The Search

"A worthy woman, *who can find?*" Is it easy to find one? The writer of Ecclesiastes longed for such a woman; "'Here is what I have found,' says the Preacher, 'adding one thing to another, to find out the reason: Which my soul still seeks, but I cannot find; One man among a thousand I have found: But a woman among all these I have not found'" (Ecc 7.27–28 NKJV). *"Who can find?"* brings to mind Abraham's desire that his son, Isaac, find a God fearing wife.

Abraham placed such importance on this mission that he sent his esteemed servant, Eliezer, to Mesopotamia to find one. He did not want Isaac to disobey God's command and marry a Canaanite who might turn his heart "to serve other gods." (See also Deut 7.1–4) Genesis 24 relates how Eliezer found Rebecca for Isaac.

Years later, true to his father's example, Isaac gave the same instructions to his own son, Jacob: "Thou shalt not take a wife of the daughters of Canaan" (Gen 28.1). Jacob's twin brother Esau's actions, and the grievous effect his idolatrous wives had on Jacob, Isaac, and Rebekah's lives showed the wisdom in God's instructions (Gen 26.34–35; 27.46). "Whoso findeth a wife findeth a good thing, and obtaineth favor of Jehovah" (Prov 18.22).

A Woman's Worth

Has your party hostess ever sent you on a scavenger hunt? If so, you can sympathize with many women today. Rushing frantically, pressured by deadlines, gathering a piece here and a piece there, but never quite getting it all together. Much of the search is centered around finding herself. She questions her identity, her purpose in life—even her worth. Proverbs 31.10–31 contains many valuable clues to help in the quest for worthy womanhood.

A woman's worth has many dimensions. The challenges and responsibilities facing her in different realms are mind-boggling at times. For example, homemaking: it takes grit and gumption to keep a home running smoothly. It takes strength, ingenuity, unselfishness, patience, and persistence to conquer the tasks that hound the homemaker. Her worth is sometimes calculated according to practical categories such as caregiver, nurse, cook, dietitian, housekeeper, laundress, seamstress, and chauffeur. This comes to an impressive amount. But does the tally even come close to the full worth of a wife and mother?

How do you determine the intangibles? Who can assess the excellence and artistry that create a warm, secure home? What price can be placed on love and sacrifice with a willing spirit? Can anyone compute kindness, integrity, resourcefulness, and perseverance? How about the faith, wisdom, courage, and common sense needed to bring up stable children in an unstable society? Where does quality time in quantity rank on the wage scale?

What mind can calculate the value of the souls of one's family and the resulting responsibility? What is the worth of years of attempting to instill values that others attempt to invalidate? Can anyone estimate the price of the sobering knowledge that the lives we choose to live affect the lives of our families and others from today through forever?

"Far Above Rubies"

The inspired writer didn't assess the worth of a worthy woman in statistical dollars and cents, but in words that made her value vivid. Her worth was appraised and it was proclaimed that "her price is far above rubies." This six-word assessment continues to impress since the ruby is still considered one of the rarest, and in large size, costliest of precious gems.

Wilson's *Old Testament Word Studies* defines rubies as "precious stones cut into several little square facets, and exquisitely polished so as to reflect beautifully at every point." This also describes a worthy woman who polishes every facet of her being into a splendid reflection of her worth.

Some seem obsessed with a person's worth. They mean money. But scripture reveals a woman's true value. "Let it be the hidden man of the heart, in the incorruptible apparel of a meek and quiet spirit, which is in the sight of God of great price" (1 Pet 3.4). A stash of rubies in a clay pot in a niche in the thick walls of the worthy woman's house didn't determine her "price." It was the stash in her heart.

In the 1600s, centuries since Proverbs 31.10 appraised and praised the worthy woman's worth, the Hope Diamond was discovered in India. Even the value of this exquisite blue, 45.5 carat diamond, for fifty years at home in the Smithsonian Institute, cannot compare with the value of a worthy woman. Her worth doesn't hang as a dazzling display from a diamond-encrusted chain. It lies at home in her heart.

Today many jewels are designed to dazzle, but the worth of a worthy woman surpasses them all. Her value is determined by worth—not wealth. Who can improve upon the words of the inspired writer? Her price is "far above rubies."

Questions

1. What are three qualities of a worthy woman's character as defined by "worthy," " excellent," or "virtuous"?

2. Who sets the standard for a "far above rubies" character? (1 Pet. 1.15–16; Eph 5.1; Rom 12.1–2)

3. Is a "worthy woman" a rare find today?

4. How do you "approve the things that are excellent"? (Phil. 1.10)

Strength Training

1. The worthy woman's inner strength motivates us to an inner workout. At home this week choose one of God's qualities to grow in.

2. Plan a daily workout using your choice.

3. As you grow in this quality, notice how it affects your relationship with God. With family. With fellow Christians. With others.

4. Exercise your realization of your worth to God. If no one else ever tells you they appreciate you, you are valuable, or loved, tell yourself, "I am valuable. I am loved." "For God so loved the world that he gave his only begotten son..." For each of us. Humbling and uplifting.

5. Study what 1 Peter 2.9–10 tells Christians about worth. Belonging. Purpose. Being special.

Worthy Woman
Ruth

Ruth, a young widow, bravely chose to leave her homeland and the gods of her people, the Moabites, and follow her God fearing mother-in-law, Naomi, to Bethlehem. There, she also made wise choices. She continued to choose the one true God as her God. She chose industry over self-pity. She chose kindness and compassion in her words and behavior toward others. She chose to listen to sound advice. She chose not to follow after "young men, whether rich or poor."

Ruth's choices prompted Boaz, a respected man in the city, to praise her saying, "All the city of my people doth know that thou art a worthy woman" (Ruth 3.11). Ruth made courageous, life-changing choices that would bring her "full reward." Are we making wise choices? How is our influence known in "all the city"? Are there gods we need to leave behind? Do we choose the one true God who will reward us in our cities on earth and in the heavenly city to come? (Psa 97.9)

Facets
The Cedar Chest

As the polish I rub into the worn wood chest brings up the reddish grain, it also brings up memories of my mother and her blend of inner and outer strength. In her thirties she and Dad packed five-year-old me, two older brothers, one spotted dog, and a sturdy, homemade wooden chest into an uncomplaining Model A Ford.

The cedar chest held our best belongings, including wool blankets, a Bird of the States quilt, and dad's old violin. We left my mother's large, South Dakota family to "go west," a dream of my dad's, and eventually settled in Southern Oregon in a small wood house backed by a deep pine forest and fronted by a field.

One April morning when I was eight, dad left for work and my brothers and I walked the three miles of dirt road to the two-room Oak Grove schoolhouse. Meanwhile, as my mother baked bread in the hot wood stove oven, sparks from the chimney burned into the roof. The smell of smoke won out over the smell of baking bread just as she saw the first flames.

She picked up my two-year-old sister, ran to put her in a car frame in the field, then raced back to the burning house. Straining with her slender 5'5" frame and choking on smoke, she dragged the heavy wooden chest out the door just before the crackling fire burned down the walls behind her. The forest rangers quickly followed the smoke, arriving in time to shovel dirt on the smoldering ashes to keep the flare-ups from spreading to field and forest.

Watching from their seat on the cedar chest that now held our only belongings were my little sister, her brown eyes wide with fright, and my mother, her trembling, drained body belieing her inner and outer strength.

TWO

The heart of her husband trusteth in her.
And he shall have no lack of gain.

Verse 10 impresses with the worthy woman's "far above rubies" heart. Now, verse 11 presents her state of the hearts marriage. "The heart of her husband trusteth in her…." His heart is safe with her heart. We begin to see how her strength of character forms a stable base for each relationship in her life.

First Place

Proverbs 31.10–31 easily divides into the basic relationships of the worthy woman's life. Her husband's heart places first—before children, home-related work, and the poor and needy. Titus 2.3–6 shows the same order. "Love their husbands" is the steady base for "love their children," home-keeping, and kindness toward others. First Peter 3.1–7 also gives importance to a husband's place in his wife's heart.

Heart to Heart

Even when a wife understands the importance of her husband's heart, the practical perspective can take over. If his clothes are clean and his stomach full, she's done. But how about his heart? Wives can forever analyze their own feelings and forget husbands have feelings too. They also have dreams and disappointments.

Do you give your husband's feelings regular attention or just toss them a thought once in awhile? Do the children's wants always come first? Whose interests and anxieties does your heart respond to quickest? Friends, extended family, or his? Heart care is essential to a happy marriage. Your husband needs someone to talk to, confide in, and be comforted by. So do you. When there is heart to heart communication the rapport ripens.

Fill in the Blanks

Communication is more than conversation. Conversation can be just a rundown of routine domestic details or always center around the children and their activities as if the children are being used to fill in the blanks in the parents' relationship. Children are special to a marriage, but in normal circumstances, they shouldn't take all of a husband and wife's time and energy. Still, loving care for infants and children can require intense and immediate attention.

When our twin sons were born, we had a ten-year-old daughter, an eight-year-old son, and a seventeen-and-a-half-month old baby. Three in diapers. No time to pamper my husband. His work schedule bulged the same time as my twin-loaded tummy, but he was especially helpful during the late night and early morning hours after they arrived. These episodes of feeding, changing, and getting babies back to sleep stretched into months of short nights of shattered sleep.

We were a sleepy, rundown, pre-dawn duo; exhausted, irritable, but still in love—when we had time to think about it. A stable, unselfish man realizes the children have to come first at times, but he knows if you still hold him first in your heart.

A husband sometimes fears that when his wife picks up their new baby she will drop her husband. It happens. One woman wrote me, "My biggest mistake was putting these helpless little darlings before Daddy, and I didn't realize it." When wives lavish all their attention and affection on the babies and their growing years, husband and wife grow apart. They no longer know each other.

Getting to Know You

Do you know your husband's heart? If you need to update, think back to your dating days. You wanted to know his thoughts, dreams, and feelings. You couldn't wait to talk to him. Is there the same enthusiasm and interest now? Being a husband, a parent, and a Christian brings growth and change. Jobs and other life experiences also add new dimensions. Do you know your here and now husband?

The delightful Rodgers-Hammerstein hit "Getting to Know You" is a refreshing approach to a renewed relationship with your husband. "Getting to know you. Getting to know all about you. Getting to like you. Getting to hope you like me." Getting to know your husband's heart and opening yours to him develops a deep bond that makes the dating days seem shallow and dull.

The knowing and growing process creates mental, emotional, and spiritual oneness—a most precious part of marriage. The longer the marriage, the greater the store of personal knowledge, romantic memories, and private jokes becomes. Years together fill the emotional storehouse with sentimental souvenirs of times both happy and sad, tense and tender. It holds timeless reminders of burdens shared and lightened by the sharing. Time takes draining, exasperating experiences and makes them funny. In the words of Edgar A. Guest, it's a "Heap O' Livin'."

Those who bail out of their marriage miss out. It takes time to build a close, rewarding relationship. Years together shouldn't sour a marriage, but make it sweeter and more serene. Serene doesn't mean dull. Time builds up an electricity that doesn't short out. People who are in a dead battery marriage often think a new mate will recharge it. Why not spark up the old marriage instead and create closeness?

Closed

A wife feels frustrated when her husband closes his heart to her. Some men pride themselves on being the "strong, silent type." Feminists and psychologists sometimes blame this type on the traditional role of men, a popular scapegoat when a man feels tears or tenderness toward his wife aren't masculine.

But, opening God's word opens hearts. The husband of Ephesians 5.28–29 "loves," "nourishes," and "cherishes," his wife. 1 Peter 3.7 also enlightens husbands and benefits wives. "Husbands, likewise, dwell with them with understanding, giving honor to the wife…" (NKJV). Husbands who want to please God and their wives eagerly honor, learn to know, and show tenderness toward them.

Elkanah

Elkanah is an example of a husband who wanted to understand and communicate his love to his wife. Hannah grieved because she had no children. Peninnah sharpened Hannah's sorrow by ridiculing her barren womb. Elkanah took Hannah's tears, her lack of appetite, and her heart to his heart and said, "Hannah, why do you weep? Why do you not eat? And why is your heart grieved?" He then tugged at her heart saying, "Am I not better to you than ten sons?" (1 Sam 1.1–8, NKJV). (See Worthy Woman Hannah)

The Bible doesn't portray a macho male image that tears or tenderness would betray. Today a man whose strength and masculinity include being loving, compassionate, and insightful is often a God-fearing man who studies the scriptures.

Boxes and bottles often carry the words, "For best results follow the manufacturers' directions." This is also important advice for a close husband-wife relationship. God created man, woman, and marriage and the written instructions to go with them. The more carefully we follow them, the better the results will be.

Trustworthy

"The heart of her husband trusteth in her." Here in verse 11 trust means "… To confide, to place hope and confidence in…" (WOWS). The worthy woman's husband trusted his heart with her in every area.

Sometimes a wife craves an open, heart to heart communication, but her husband hangs a closed sign on his heart. If the sign is newly hung out, lack of trust may be the reason. Maybe his wife betrayed him when he trusted his feelings with her.

Has your husband ever confided a sensitivity to you, then you poked fun at him about it in public? If he admits to a blunder at work, do you help him feel stupid? When he does squeak out an apology, do you use it against him? Do you stir him up to take a stand, then withdraw your support? Do you whine about his weaknesses to gain sympathy from friends or family? Being untrustworthy with his feelings and confidences can hammer up a closed sign in a hurry.

Trust is essential to the marriage commitment. Marriage is a trust company in which husband and wife are in full partnership. It isn't just an agreement put together by two people, according to their own terms, and subject to their own decision to continue or terminate it. The marriage covenant binds husband and wife together for a lifetime of love and trust.

"No Longer Two"

God ordained marriage to be a lifelong union between one man and one woman; a lifetime commitment to oneness. "But from the beginning of the creation, God made them male and female. For this reason a man shall leave his father and mother and be joined to his wife, and the two shall become one flesh; so then they are no longer two, but one flesh. Therefore what God has joined together, let not man separate. …Whoever divorces his wife and marries another commits adultery against her. And if a woman divorces her husband and marries another, she commits adultery" (Mark 10.6–12, NKJV).

When a marriage is miserable, some think it's easier to become two again than to work for a wonderful oneness. They rush from the realization of the sad state of their marriage to the rationalization that they have "irreconcilable differences." They "can't take it anymore." One or both decide to break their vows "to have and to hold from this day forward, for better, for worse, for richer, for poorer, in sickness and in health, to love and to cherish, til death do us part."

Matthew 19.9 gives fornication as a reason for divorce, but many flee for flimsy reasons. "I'm not happy." "I want more."

"She's boring." "He doesn't excite me." Do the wedding vows come with "Perfection guaranteed or your vows will be voided"?

"God hates divorce" (Mal 2.16). Yet husbands and wives sometimes treat divorce like the flu. "We'll feel yucky for awhile, but we'll get over it." They then self-diagnose with divorce rather than faithfully following God's prescription: "Therefore what God has joined together, let not man separate" (Matt 19.6, NKJV).

Are God's "special people" (1 Pet 2.9) becoming the same as society with its easy acceptance of divorce? Taking the weak way out? Letting selfishness and impatience pound down perseverance instead of building caring and closeness? Rather than being apart through separation or divorce, why not nobly embrace "I can do all things in him that strengthens me" (Phil 4.13) along with each other? It is a fearsome thing to break the family circle.

In one sad case a man's wife left him and their children to follow another man, where life seemed easier and more exciting. Later, their father married a woman who also was deserted along with her children. A few years later an accident took his life. His children didn't want the mother who had left them to come to their father's funeral. So she sent a standing, heart-shaped red and white arrangement to the small country cemetery. When the children learned the deer ate the flowers off her arrangement, they laughed. They were older now, but still hurting and resentful. The sinful, selfish, short-sighted "it's my life" causes children life-long pain.

Too Hard?

It takes faith to put a depressing marriage in God's hands and trust Him to help you save it, but "Is anything too hard for Jehovah?" (Gen 18.14). When a marriage is in crisis it takes strength and wisdom to make the children's hearts a priority. Parents who want their children to learn love must model it for them. How can they teach forgiveness if they won't forgive each other? Will children learn the lessons of 1 Corinthians 13 if parents allow impatience, unkindness, pride, selfishness, and anger to lead to the life-altering damage of divorce to their children's lives?

Sadly, many husbands and wives don't choose to know and grow together. They obsess on other interests then say, "We've grown apart." They begin to disdain their mate and claim their marriage is unbearable. God can bear them up and give them wisdom and endurance to do the head work, heart work, and hard work it will take to make their marriage work.

"No temptation has overtaken you except such as is common to man; but God is faithful, who will not allow you to be tempted beyond what you are able, but with the temptation will also make the way of escape, that you may be able to bear it" (1 Cor 10.13, NKJV). God is faithful. You are able. "If any of you lacks wisdom, let him ask of God, who gives to all liberally and without reproach, and it will be given to him" (Jas 1.5, NKJV).

If the time, energy, and mental, emotional and physical strength that are dissipated through divorce are put into the marriage, can it not be saved? Will divorce bring peace and eliminate stress? Divorce usually brings strain and pain over alimony, child custody, child support, distraught children, switching children back and forth between parents' houses, in-law overlap, mutual funds and mutual friends.

And if one takes a new mate there are new problems to add to the old ones. Choosing to dissolve the marriage instead of solving the problems brings a new marriage and more maladjustment. Heaping all of this upon the sinfulness of the situation doesn't spell "happily ever after." In such cases, the second marriage often ends the same way as the first.

Studying and living by the word of the all wise God who "has joined together" will help husband and wife not only stay together but be ever thankful they are "no longer two."

"One Flesh"

In considering trust, it seems suitable to consider the sexual union between husband and wife. First, they should bring purity to their marriage, then continue to keep themselves for each other only. God created sexual desires and designed marriage between man and woman as the honorable realm for them to be fulfilled.

"Let marriage be had in honor among all, and let the bed be undefiled; for fornicators and adulterers God will judge" (Heb 13.4).

The sexual relationship is meant to be lovingly looked forward to by both husband and wife. Love is central to lovemaking. The sweet communion between husband and wife includes both mind and body. A loving husband wants to understand and please his wife, and a loving wife responds with passion and tenderness. Principles discussed earlier that affect emotional closeness also apply to physical closeness.

Being physically or emotionally drained affects lovemaking. The wedding night can be disappointing when bride and groom are tense, tired, and emotionally exhausted from the wedding and related events, and stressful preparations preceding them. The tension and fatigue are mutually understood and remembered with humor. But if the same pattern is repeated as the years go by, it is no longer funny.

Emergencies happen. Schedules get overcrowded. Over planning and bursts of busyness can leave the wife drained, but if this is the usual routine, her husband feels rejected. He trusts his feelings and desires with her and his passion is turned to hurt pride and frustration. A wife's desire and response affects her husband's feeling of masculinity and self-image. And his expressiveness, or lack of, affects her.

If a wife has to beg for her husband's "I love you" or tender touches, she will be less stirred by them and will resent him for her own deflated ego and feeling of being unloved. She can then be tempted to drag out some imaginary girlhood "dream guy" that no real guy could live up to to fill the void. If emotional energies are wasted on a figment of the imagination or fantasizing about someone else, she can't cleave to her real, live husband.

Grudge Sludge

Anger can annihilate affection. If he leaves for work so angry he wonders why he married, and she is furious because he left a sloppy mess in the bathroom for her to wade through, the wrong kind of sparks will fly. Given the short-circuit effect that minor grievances can have on marriage, it's easy to see how bitterness that has been boiling along for years can contribute to a power outage.

But husband and wife can reach into the Ephesians 4.31–32 medicine chest and throw out the bottled up "bitterness, and wrath, and anger, and clamor, and railing... and all malice," and keep the healing "be ye kind one to another, tenderhearted, forgiving each other, even as God also in Christ forgave you." Taken with humility for the required time, they will heal wounds and restore a healthy, loving relationship.

Respect also affects sexual intimacy. 1 Peter 3.7 tells the husband to honor his wife. Ephesians 5.33 tells the wife to respect her husband. An attitude of respect ripens romance more than arrogance and resentment that decrease desire. Constant criticism or ridicule is devastating to the marriage relationship, including the sexual union. An ego that is verbally assaulted isn't eager to take further risks at failure. A vicious cycle then begins that leads to further sin.... " Do not deprive one another... so that Satan does not tempt you" (1 Cor 7.2–5, NKJV). Earlier we saw the importance of getting to know your husband. On the subject of sex, think "know," not "No."

The Bible can't be blamed for the idea that sex is something a husband demands and his wife tolerates. Sex also isn't threat or bribe power to hang over your bed to win your way in other matters. The sexual union is a God designed gift to both husband and wife. Both should be warm, willing, and trustworthy with this gift.

Untrustworthy

Proverbs contains many examples of and warnings about the immoral, loose, strange, or evil woman, so it seems important in discussing trust to consider her devastating effect on home and family. "This is the way of an adulterous woman: She eats and wipes her mouth, and says 'I have done no wickedness' (Prov 30.20). Some adulterous women think immorality is fun, and tell themselves "I have done no wrong" (NASB). Misled by their conscience and others' standards, many immoral women haven't matured past the peer pressure of "Everybody's doing it," to responsibility and consequences.

Scripture doesn't single out single women. Adulterous means married. Either can do evil. An immoral woman may seem confident, successful, and knowing, but "Her ways are unstable and she knoweth it not" (Prov 5.6). Often women who condone, promote, or are involved in immorality, such as premarital sex, adultery, pornography, lesbianism, and prostitution profess to be open-minded intellectuals, but Romans 1.22 puts it this way: "Who professing to be wise they became fools." Seceond Timothy 3.6–7 speaks of "gullible women loaded down with sins, led away by various lusts, always learning and never able to come to the knowledge of the truth" (NKJV).

Proverbs 11.22 warns of something more pandemic than the swine flu. "As a ring of gold in a swine's snout, so is a lovely woman who lacks discretion." Worldwide, the beauty of womanhood is often wasted on indiscreet women who root in the mud of immorality as a pig with a ring of gold in its snout would use it to root in the mud.

Proverbs 7 gives a sin by sin account of an untrustworthy wife's part in the downfall of a foolish young man who chose to yield to her persuasion. Verse 10, (NKJV) describes both her inner and outer attire. "With the attire of a harlot, and a crafty heart..." Her clothing exposed her intention just as a woman's clothing today suggests what she is about. Her actions carried out the promise of her outfit. Her cunning heart caused her to be adept at deceit and an accomplished flirt as she diligently sought to snare her victim. She was "loud and rebellious." "Her feet" would not stay at home (v 11).

"So she caught him and kissed him." And, shamelessly, even used her observance of religious practices in her scheme to seduce him (vv 13–15). Next, she described her seductive setup of comfortable cushions and perfumed bed, then issued the invitation: "Come, let us take our fill of love until morning." Now comes the clincher. "For my husband is not at home; he has gone on a long journey" (vv 18–19).

This adulterous woman manipulated the young man with "enticing speech" and "flattering lips," then used the luxuries her husband had probably brought her from business trips to snare him. "The heart of her husband" definitely could not trust in her.

Maybe he was gone a lot. Maybe he was preoccupied, and she felt lonely and unloved. But did her circumstances cause her to sin? Or was it her weak character? It was her heart. "He that hath a wayward heart, findeth no good." (Prov 17.20). A trustworthy woman would have used herself and her home in worthy ways.

A Full Soul

"The full soul loatheth a honeycomb, but to the hungry soul every bitter thing is sweet" (Prov 27.7). The immoral woman won't appeal to the husband whose "soul is full." His wife can create a void that makes him vulnerable. Does she set him up for sin, or satisfy him as only a wife can? A Twinkie or a doughnut isn't as tempting when the stomach is full, and neither is a cheap thrill to a fulfilled husband. A wise wife loves her husband and lets him know it.

"Boys Will Be Boys"?

"Don't even think about it," says Proverbs 5.3–9 to the man who ponders following an immoral woman down the path of fornication. "Lest you ponder her path of life." "Remove your way far from her." "Her steps lay hold of hell" (v 5, NKJV). The man who "touches" his neighbor's wife is also condemned (Prov 6.29 NKJV).

Even if his wife rejects him, the trustworthy husband will reject the advances of the immoral woman. A loving wife strengthens her husband's armor against her, but he must fortify himself. "Put on the whole armor of God, that ye may be able to stand against the wiles of the devil" (Eph 6.11). Joseph provides an excellent example of wisdom over wiles (Gen 39.7–12).

A wife may give and respond to her husband in every way, but he seeks out sin. "A worthless man deviseth mischief" (Prov 16.27). Scripture shows that immoral men are just as guilty of sin and ignorance as immoral women. "And knoweth not that it is for his life" (Prov 6.32; 7.23). Solomon said, "I find more bitter than death the woman whose heart is snares and nets and whose hands are bands; whoso pleaseth God shall escape from her; but the sinner shall be taken by her" (Ecc 7.26). There is no "boys will be boys" leeway in the Bible.

"Always"

In contrast to an adulterous relationship or a sleazy one-night stand, Proverbs 5.15–23 shows the blessings of a lifetime of faithfulness. Marriage provides a lifelong joy and excitement for husband and wife in which the sexual relationship plays an important part. Verse 18 says "rejoice in the wife of thy youth." Verse 19, "… be thou ravished always with her love." Does that sound like a wife is something her husband is just stuck with? "Rejoice," and "be ravished." Be transported. Be excited and delighted by her love. Boredom unlimited? Dutiful toleration? No. Take extreme pleasure. "Be exhilarated." "Always."

It might be unrealistic to expect Fourth of July fireworks every day, but a loving, lasting marriage provides a steady, serene base for regular explosions of romance and excitement throughout one's lifetime. Bible-taught fidelity may seem like an overly principled approach to some, but it brings rich rewards to the faithful husband and wife.

Many fail at marriage or don't want to learn the laws of the one who designed it, then announce it obsolete. You don't throw out the judicial system because you can't pass the bar exam.

Hebrews 13.4 pronounces marriage honorable, not obsolete. A stable, happy marriage is a "till death do us part" depository of richness and romance that live-in lovers can only dream of.

"No Lack of Gain"

The worthy woman's husband trusts his heart, home, and possessions with her. She not only proves worthy of that trust, *"He shall have no lack of gain."* Just as victory in war reaps gain for the man of battle, winning a wife with the qualities of the worthy woman brings gain to the fortunate husband in many areas of his life. First, lets consider the financial.

There are many money traps. Proverbs 30.8–9 shows the rich can feel satisfied and forget God, and the poor can be tempted to steal and feel justified in doing so. Rich or poor can be obsessed with money; getting it, increasing it, using it, or the fear of losing it. Trying to deceive people into thinking they have more money than they do can also consume a marriage.

"Now godliness with contentment is great gain" (1 Tim 6.6). A godly woman with a contented heart is less likely to fall into the "love of money" trap or give her husband a shove into it. This evil entrapment can cause husband and wife to put money or the luxuries and fun it affords before the Lord, their relationship, and their children. When husband and wife deplete themselves physically and emotionally pursuing riches, the spiritual and family life can become impoverished. "Do not overwork to be rich" (Prov 23.4 NKJV).

Millions of married couples meet the small income or job loss challenge with faith, thrift, ingenuity, patience, and sacrifice. Others give up or let conflicting goals, poor spending habits, greed, selfishness, or unrealistic expectations cause chaos. Young marrieds sometimes expect to enjoy the same lifestyle as their parents who worked and waited years before achieving their level of comfort.

The trustworthy wife strives to make the most of her husband's assets and earnings. She is patiently realistic so that he doesn't deplete his health and resources trying to meet unreasonable demands. Someone once said, "Whether a man ends up with a nest egg or a goose egg often depends on the chick he married." The husband can be the unwise, impulsive spender who overestimates their income, or prefers the "ignorance is bliss" approach. This puts an added burden on his wife as she tries to balance their budget with respect for her husband. Sometimes the wife eagerly accepts the task of budgeting, then spends their money on her own interests and activities so fast it melts the plastic.

When a trusting husband and a trustworthy wife put their trust in God and pray and plan together, working as one, they will enjoy the "gain" He blesses them with. "God gives us richly all things to enjoy" (1 Tim 6.17).

There are many areas in Proverbs 31.10–31 where a wife can bring her husband gain or "lack of gain." One is his reputation. If she doesn't have his best interest at heart, or if she is immoral, or offensive, she can harm his reputation in the church, community, with his work, or wherever he is known. (See "in the gates" – ch 9)

He should also be able to trust her as they train their children, knowing her example, teaching, friends, and activities will reflect mutual values and contribute to the welfare of their home. A worthy woman's husband can trust his heart and home with her for, as we see next in chapter 3, "She does him good and not evil" (NKJV).

Questions

1. What are some ways that knowing his wife is trustworthy affects a husband?

2. How does 2 Timothy 3.16–17 apply to God's word regarding marriage? Did God design His word with a delete button?

3. How do modern marriage contracts or prenuptial agreements usually view the permanency of marriage? What is the potential for a "If it doesn't work out" marriage?

4. How can what we read or watch make us vulnerable to temptation?

5. Why is godliness important to a husband's and wife's contentment?

Strength Training

Privately, consider:

1. Based on what you tell others about your husband, would they like and respect him?

2. Is there a weak area in your trustworthiness? With God's word as your personal trainer, begin to strengthen it. Is this something you and your husband can work on together?

3. Most marriages experience "growing pains." Are you and your husband growing closer together or farther apart?

4. Do you really know your here and now husband? Are you aware of and interested in his "new growth"?

5. Weight lift with your wedding albums. Focus on your bride and groom pictures. What were your dreams and goals then for family, fun, spiritual, and financial areas? Do you still share mutual goals?

6. Plan a dinner date to talk about your dreams and goals and work out a plan together.

Worthy Woman
Hannah

With aching heart Hannah traveled from her hill country home to Shiloh with her husband Elkanah, and his other wife, Peninnah, for the yearly sacrifice. Each year Peninnah, blessed with sons and daughters, ridiculed Hannah because she was barren. Peninnah's cruelty deepened Hannah's heartache; "therefore, she wept and did not eat." Elkanah, "who loved Hannah," was moved by her tears, her lack of appetite, and her grieving heart, to try to comfort her.

In deep sorrow, Hannah turned to God. Weeping, she worded a silent, anguished prayer that revealed something central to her character: humility. She pleaded for God to "Look on the affliction of thy handmaid… ," and again, "forget not thy handmaid." She humbly vowed that if God would give her a son, she would give him back to God. She didn't allow bitterness to cause her to rail against Peninnah or against God, but rather begged for His blessing as His servant.

At the temple, during Hannah's heartfelt prayer, Eli the priest saw that her lips moved but her voice was silent. He thought she was drunk and rebuked her. Even at false accusation in the midst of misery, Hannah showed humility and respect. "No, my Lord, I am a woman of sorrowful spirit." She also showed that a servant attitude can include self-respect, as she humbly defended herself. "I have drunk neither wine nor strong drink, but I poured out my soul before Jehovah. Count not thy handmaid for a wicked woman."

Eli bid Hannah peace and an answer from God to her prayers. She asked favor from Eli for his "handmaid." In her grief she sought God, and now her faith in Him glowed in her peaceful composure as she "went her way, and did eat."

Back at home Hannah conceived and bore Samuel. When he was weaned she took him to Eli. There her words showed she had not shed her humility once her prayer was answered. "Oh, my lord. ...For this child I prayed; and Jehovah hath given me my petition." She had wept and prayed for God to give her this son, now she did not weep and pray to keep him. True to her vow she "granted him to Jehovah."

Hannah left her young child Samuel with Eli, then again turned to prayer. This time her heart rejoiced as she praised God who continued to bless them as the child Samuel "grew before Jehovah," and with two more sons and daughters. While we remember Peninnah only for her cruelty and pride, the prayerful, devoted Hannah lives on in our hearts as a worthy woman of deep humility (1 Sam 1.1–2.11).

Facets
The Simple Things

The simple things profoundly impact the husband and wife life. Simple things that husband and wife do for each other cheer their hearts and strengthen their marriage. Husbands thrive on the things their wives do that show love and respect, such as kind words of caring and encouragement. They appreciate clean, pressed clothes needed to help them meet deadlines, and the love note tucked in a pocket, suitcase, or laid on the driver's seat.

His favorite dish cooked to congratulate or console warms more than his stomach, and he too enjoys thoughtful cards and gifts for special occasions. He feels welcomed and refreshed by a house that doesn't seem like he is stepping from one whirlwind into another, and by the playfulness and sense of humor that makes years of marriage still feel like fun. Knowing he is high on your prayer list heartens him, and he is buoyed when you know what lifts him up when he is down.

Wives too appreciate the simple things that have a big effect on their need to feel loved and honored. Each wife is unique and it delights her when her husband tries to understand and please her. My husband knows that when the bulbs start breaking the cold ground in the Oregon springtime, I get the urge to do the same. He also knows from 53 years of seeing me plant and pamper my nursery finds, that when the soil warms, I would rather have a simple box of bedding plants than a bouquet of florist-fresh flowers. These days he digs the larger holes for planting, moves the heavier patio pots, and prunes the roses during our cold Februarys. He shows love in other simple ways, from loading the dishwasher to picking up groceries.

About 3:30 one morning my sleep apnea machine woke me. Al also woke up and slipped out to the office about 5:00 AM. Weighed down by some family concerns, and the same ten pounds I had lost three times before, I dragged myself to the kitchen. There on the countertop was a note. I picked it up, and feeling like a living nightmare, read "You are my dreams come true"—a simple, timely, spirit-lifter from a loving, knowing husband.

Thoughtfulness and romance aren't limited by budget. Imagination is free. Even the simplest lifestyle is filled with opportunities to love and lift each other through life, caring, sharing, and doing the simple things.

THREE

She doeth him good and not evil
All the days of her life.

The minute the bride says "I do" she begins to do her husband "good." A wife who does her husband "good and not evil" is a helper in harmony with his very being as she assists and completes him. "And Jehovah God said, It is not good that the man should be alone; I will make him a help meet for him."

Genesis 2.18–25 gives an eloquent account of God's knowledge of man's need, His creation of woman to meet that need, His presentation of her to the man, and the man's response upon receiving her. Woman was an original creation that made possible a perfect oneness. God created a woman and presented her to the man Himself. She came special delivery!

He received God's gift saying, "This is now bone of my bones, and flesh of my flesh; she shall be called Woman because she was taken out of Man." Proverbs 19.14 states, "A prudent wife is from Jehovah." As his gift "from Jehovah," a worthy woman does her husband "good…" (Prov 31.12).

Networking

In the New Testament God gives women a special system to help them do "good." As always, God was ahead of the times with this ancient, yet up-to-date networking system: the older women are to be "teachers of that which is good; that they may train the young women to love their husbands, to love their children, to be soberminded, chaste, workers at home, kind, being in subjection to their own husbands, that the word of God be not blasphemed" (Tit 2.3–5). Following this format, older women give the younger support, encouragement, and time-tested teaching in being godly women, wives, and mothers.

The younger women appreciate the older women as they realize the older were once the younger who were striving to learn and live the qualities of Titus 2.4–5. They've been there. Think of the growth that takes place in this cycle. Older women studied and struggled as they learned the lessons of verses 4–5 as younger women. Now, as the older women, they are to live the lives of verse 3 so that their good example enables them to teach the younger women "that which is good." As they "admonish" the younger women they are "teachers of good things" (NKJV). They set in motion a far-reaching network of nurture.

When older women in a congregation counsel, comfort, and guide in loving, motherly ways, and the younger women respond as loving daughters would, all benefit. The benefits are felt, not only in the homes, but in the congregation.

Sharing and caring—not just older to older and younger to younger, but also older to younger, and younger to older—then you have a motherly-daughterly-sisterly relationship, a unique closeness as sisters-in-Christ. Within this circle of sisters there is a family feeling of belonging, help, warmth, and fun as they thrive on the Titus 2 network of learning, and teaching, and living "that which is good."

Show and Tell

Proverbs 31.10–31 provides a timeless "how to" from the Old Testament for doing "good." Titus 2.3–5 provides a New Testament parallel. These sections of scripture complement each other as they equip today's woman with picturesque illustrations from Proverbs 31 and straightforward teaching from Titus 2 to help young women know and do "that which is good."

Verses 4 and 5 of Titus 2 explain what this "good" is. Let's look at them in list form.

- Love their husband
- Love their children
- Be sober-minded
- Be chaste
- Be workers at home
- Be kind
- Be in subjection to their husbands
- Word of God be not blasphemed

First Timothy 5.14 also highlights the home sphere as it tells the young widowed women to regain a life based on the same elements as Titus 2.4–5. The qualifications of the "widow indeed" in 1 Timothy 5.9–10 are also set around husband, children, home, and others, giving the life of an older godly woman in retrospect.

Once, while reading the above passages during a long wait in a car, their similarities seemed to jump out at me. I was also struck by the difference between the Bible verses and what seemed to be happening in society. The following chart is the result of those reflections.

Titus 2	vs.	Society
Love husband		Love self
Love children		Leave children
Sober-minded		Foolish
Chaste		Immoral
Workers at home		Go to work
Be kind		Be selfish
Be in subjection		Be your own boss
Word of God not blasphemed		Irreverent toward Bible

This chart helps us explore "that which is good" of Titus 2.3–5 while being alert to the life of the Proverbs 31 woman who does her husband "good." We will only consider four of the points since the others fit naturally in other chapters.

Titus Two Says "Love Their Husband"

Titus 2.4–5 lists the things the young wives were to do. "Love their husbands" heads the list.

Phileo, the Greek word for love in verse 4, is a tender, affectionate love. It doesn't leave your husband wondering. He feels secure in your love, not unsure. *Phileo* love prompts kind words and tender touches that show him marriage doesn't end romance but rather, places you both in the God-designed sphere for affection to flourish.

If the turn-on turns off when you discover your chosen one isn't perfect—*Phileo* to the rescue! *Phileo* love empathizes and overlooks his faults. "Love is blind" is a dangerous approach to choosing a husband. A "big man on campus" kind of guy may not make a "known in the gates" kind of husband. A way with words and an appealing physical appearance can also blind you to a man's spiritual stature.

But once you marry, put on the love-colored glasses. Look at your husband with the eyes of Philippians 4.8. Concentrate on his good qualities; then, together, learn to live the love of 1 Corinthians 13.4–7 and help each other be the best husband and wife you can be.

Many try a *phileo* phase—then opt out. Someone has said, "One advantage of marriage is that if you fall out of love, it keeps you together 'til you fall back in." Titus 2.4 says love can be learned and relearned; when you don't think you love him after all, when love is there but needs nourishing.

Whatever the age or stage of marriage, when you don't feel you love your husband, you usually don't act like it. Most often, when you act like it the feelings will follow, he will respond, and you will once again "love your husband"—"fall back in."

Older couples as well as young often need to learn to love each other. If the marriage wasn't based on love it will take extra hard work. If it started on a high plane, but is now experiencing love lag, it will need refueling. If it is damaged, it will take patience, forgiveness, and perseverance before love takes wings. Sensitivity, attention, and understanding will be crucial so husband and wife can once again trust each other and feel secure in their loving marriage. (See also Spiritual Oneness – ch 9)

Society Says "Love Self"

Wives sometimes switch their "love their husband" perspective to a "me first" marriage. They cheat themselves as they change their warm, loving attitude to a cool, calculating, "What's in it for me?" If husband and wife are both stuck in the selfish cycle, their marriage spins dry. First Corinthians 13.5 counsels "love seeketh not its own." Mature love doesn't seek self first.

Think of the level of love and caring possible if husband and wife live Philippians 2.4: "Not looking each of you to his own things, but each of you also to the things of others." Reading from verse 8 that Christ humbled himself, "even unto the death of the cross," makes a petty perspective seem even more selfish.

The "me first" mindset often comes with a "right now temperament." Impatience can cause us to rush ahead of the Lord and what is best for ourselves and our families. Psalm 37 slows us down. "Trust in the Lord, and do good." There's that word "good" again. "Rest in the Lord and wait patiently for him"… "Do not fret—it only causes harm" (NKJV). Fretting, which includes whining and complaining, wears us and others away. Fretting and stewing lead to evil doing.

Unselfishly doing your husband "good, and not evil," and loving him the Titus 2.3–5 way will one day reap the real rewards that exceed the superficial ones that might be gained by impatiently seeking self. "Wait on the Lord and keep his way..." (Psa 37.34 NKJV).

Titus Two Says "Love Their Children"

"A mother's specialty is loving her husband and children. Even more, just plain loving—ranging from animals to humans." Just before Mother's Day I received this quote in the mail from the thoughtful teacher of our then eleven-year-old daughter. The teacher's note read: "Lisa wrote this for her weekly paragraph. I thought you would enjoy it too." Her paragraph continued, "Sometimes we don't appreciate our Mothers as much as we should. It's easy to say that, but I for one don't appreciate mine as much as I possibly could. I'm going to start trying a little bit harder. Now, how about you?"

In the midst of maxi motherhood at the time, with five children, including three under age three, I was moved by Melisa's writing. These words from an already sweet, helpful daughter, also provided an out of the mouth of innocents definition for this section. "A mother's specialty is loving her husband and children."

Again, this is the expressive, affectionate, *phileo* love. A caring, accepting love doesn't depend on a child's beauty or high I.Q. A child isn't a status symbol to make the parents look good to others. You love your child just as much the day he clogs up the school plumbing with an orange as the day he receives the good citizenship award, though you use a different approach for each event. Love includes training and discipline as well as affection.

Showing *phileo* love comes more naturally to some than others. Mothers who are easily affectionate have usually seen their parents show affection to each other and have received and returned loving words and hugs as children. Mothers who were perhaps emotionally deprived themselves may find it harder to express their feelings, though mothers who didn't hear "I love you" as children often take extra care to express affection to their own. *Phileo* love also prompts the practical actions that make children feel loved and cared for.

Society Says "Leave Their Children"

"Raising kids is like being pecked to death by a chicken." The decorative sign in an upscale gift shop expresses the attitude of some in society; children gradually wear the life out of you, rather than being "a gift from the Lord" (Psa 127.3), they are a burden instead of a blessing. Women who feel overwhelmed by mother-hood's responsibilities are especially vulnerable to this viewpoint.

Many didn't expect the changes motherhood makes. Perhaps they enjoyed a somewhat glamorous hospital stay where mother reigned as she received gifts, visitors, and care while she rested and cuddled her sweet-smelling little bundle.

But, once at home where glamor can change to clamor, with a burpy baby, stinky diapers, and mother the major mystery solver for the wide awake crying, that "head for the hills" feeling begins to compete with the maternal instincts. Some who were dreamily launched on the sweet-pink cloud of motherly bliss are deflated by the down to earth reality of being on 24-hour alert with less energy and added expenses. Just as some seem "in love with love" until day to day living marries romance with reality, some seem in love with having children until they have to take care of them.

Becoming a parent is an eye-opener. What parent hasn't longed for a break, experienced fractured finances, or felt terminally ex-hausted? Escape or adjust? Most adjust, but some succumb to es-cape routes such as time-consuming hobbies, careers, or pleasure pursuits. Some choose a more permanent "Go-Now-Pay-Later" plan—getting them off their hands for now, only to have them hurt their hearts in the future.

Some choose being at home full time. Much can be said for full time mothering. A full time mother isn't someone who lives through her children, breathing "smother love" as she waits on their every whim; rather, she has a more on-site opportunity to love, enjoy, teach respect and responsibility, discipline, and de-velop spiritual and moral character.

Sadly, many mothers at home, or working full time, do their best for their children and still suffer heartbreak. All parents face this possibility, but there is great risk in giving too little to so large an undertaking. Our American "hurry up" way of life can cause parents to rush their children through babyhood, toddling, pre-teens, teens, and on out the door. Though you may enter this phase of life with eyes half-closed, you barely blink twice before it is over.

Titus Two Says "Workers at Home"

A wife and mother's cape of responsibility covers many areas. Letting scholars define "workers at home" shows the possible scope of the expression in Titus 2.5. Thayer's *Greek-English Lexicon of the New Testament* has "…the (watch or) keeper of the house." Vine's *Expository Dictionary of New Testament Words* gives "…Working at home, RV… Some Mss. have *ikourous*, watching or keeping the home." Vincent's *Word Studies in the New Testament* includes "Keepers or guardian of the household." Bagster's *Analytical Greek Lexicon* has "Keeper or guard of house. A home keeper. Stay at home, domestic."

Today, modern technology makes it seem time at home isn't as necessary. But can a parent be replaced? There still isn't a "Greet the Children After School" gadget or a "Sibling Squabble Settler." Has anyone invented a "Just Being There" button to listen to the fun of a child's day, encourage progress, or help ward off problems for the next? And how about moral and spiritual concepts?

With teenagers, some days you seem to just be answering what I called the "Any's." "Anything to eat?" "Any phone calls for me?" "Anything to do?" Teenagers can seem aloof to your being at home, even campaigning for more freedom, then surprise you as one 16-year-old son did one hot day. He got home from school, saw me down the street, and met me with a cup of ice water. He responded to my surprised "Thank you" with, "Well, you always have something for us when we get home."

With today's news showing drugs and alcohol use, teen violence, witchcraft and occultism, premarital sex, and abortion of grave concern, how can mothers feel they are less needed at home? Common sense says children need more time and guidance, not less.

Some working moms can adjust their schedules to their children. Many children of working moms receive careful care from family, friends, or others. Their older teens are trustworthy and responsible. But what of the young mind that sits unsupervised soaking up sex and violence on television, absorbing the filth available in offensive books, magazines, or on the internet, or running free with questionable friends? Can we "rule the house" by remote? (See also "she looketh well to – ch 12)

Society Says "Go to Work"

In contrast to Titus 2.5 society, through books, magazines, movies, newspapers, television, and the internet says to the young mother, "Go to work." Many have. Whether to work outside the home or not is a complex subject in a complex society. Circumstances and resources for help with child care vary from home to home.

Death of a spouse, family illness, financial crisis due to job loss or other misfortune drives many mothers to work. Some long for the luxury of staying home, but sad circumstances place their tired feet on a time clock treadmill, which they hope will be temporary, but often isn't. Mothers, single by choice or no choice, usually also become breadwinners.

Many work for the meaning they hope to bring to others' lives, others for the fulfillment they think a job will bring. Some see women in glamorous careers and envy the supposed satisfactions. Careers do bring excitement and satisfaction to some. Others feel the dream realized wasn't worth the trade-off for homey pleasures and opportunities missed in their eagerness to look for new ones.

The "right now" attitude can result in the "leave your children" choice. Some, impatient for financial gain, though often with the intent of giving advantages to their children, opt for careers sacrificing other advantages more lasting than the privileges enjoyed.

Some wives and mothers work part time from home in ways such as selling their artistic creations or home cooked food, computer work, giving music lessons, sewing, writing, or providing day care, working these activities around their work at home.

Their desire to be at home motivates many to save with more home cooking and less convenience foods or meals out. They also figure in money saved on child care, gas, and special clothing needed for some jobs. The dailies a wife does can create a less stressful home life that gives her husband more spirit for his work, and helps him be a more productive breadwinner. Realizing her important part adds to the satisfaction her work at home brings.

Many mothers who work outside the home have never given not working much thought. Maybe their mothers always worked or their friends and neighbors all do. Others feel their self-esteem slipping as they feel the disdain of friends or family who, convinced their homes held them in bondage, have joined the mass exodus to the marketplace.

Sometimes a homemaker tries to steady her shaky ego by "going to work." It may not be as stimulating or challenging as being at home, but she has "a job." Though she prefers to be at home, she is still living by the peer pressure gauge she warns her children against. Is she pressing herself to do more work to impress those who think her oppressed?

The husband sometimes has the "just a housewife" hang up. He feels content at home where all enjoy the benefits of his wifes time and work, but cringes when a co-worker says, "What does your wife do?" He fears she will be thought boring, or both thought old-fashioned. His attitude is crucial to his wife's. If he appreciates her being at home, but seems embarrassed, or more impressed by women co-workers, he undermines her enthusiasm. When a wife and mother is doing her best at what she knows is best for her family, hearing, "I'm proud of you," "Thank you for all you do for our home and family," heartens her for her hard work.

Titus 2 Says "Being in Subjection"

The young wife of Titus 2.4–5 learns to love her "husband" and "children," "be sober-minded," "chaste," "a worker at home," and "kind." These qualities are within an attitude of "being in subjection" to her husband, with the all-important purpose being to reflect well on God's word, that it not be "blasphemed."

Ephesians 5.22–33 shows the husband-wife relationship as God designed it to be a blessing to both: "Wives be in subjection unto your husband as unto the Lord. For the husband is the head of the wife, as Christ also is the head of the church, being himself the savior of the body. But as the church is subject to Christ, so let the wives also be to their husbands in everything.

Husbands, love your wives, even as Christ also loved the church, and gave himself up for it."

These verses sing harmony and happiness to the husband and wife when his Christ like, loving, sacrificial leadership is coupled with her loving honor and respect for him (v 33). In verse 25, the husband's love for his wife is the Greek word *Agape*. *Agape* love acts in her best interest. It doesn't speak affectionate agreement to her every whim when circumstances need both to take a realistic approach, but neither does it tell him to treat her in a matter-of-fact manner.

Instead, verses 29 and 32 tell the husband to sacrificially love, nourish, and cherish his wife and to demonstrate his love for her in unselfish, caring ways. The warm, softening approach the Greek word for "cherish" teaches her husband to have will deepen her caring and respect for him, and make her more receptive to and understanding of the purpose of subjection.

When there is an open sharing with each giving kind consideration to the others feelings and view points, a final say situation is more likely to be a non-event.

Husbands can make this concept harder to understand by seeming self-centered and preoccupied, like the 30-ish man who, oblivious to the ocean view, and with his plate off-side, forked in the food he grabbed from the lavish breakfast buffet as, sniffing the newsprint, he hunched hungrily over the sports section, relishing each morsel, crumb by savory crumb. He finally acknowledged his sidelined young wife with a few tidbits of the wins, losses, steroid suspicions, and player swaps before returning to the sports smorgasbord to lap up the leftovers. Some wives compete with computers or are benched by briefcases.

When a husband models the sacrificial leading, loving, nourishing, and cherishing concept of subjection, his wife feels appreciation and relief. Her husband's loving leadership frees her for her own unique privileges and responsibilities. She doesn't strangle her joy and creativity trying to take over his responsibilities. Rather, her respect helps him fulfill them, and her own feminine abilities and attributes flourish.

Society Says "Be Your Own Boss"

In today's society many women don't realize the God de-signed purpose of subjection. They take a "You can't make me" approach. They are right. A husband can't make his wife be in subjection. It's an inner attitude. You can mentally sneer as you physically follow through on a decision. In a final say situation you can say "Okay. If that's the way you want it," then slam doors and shoot sharp looks to let him know you don't have to like it. Sometimes a wife is outwardly agreeable while inwardly wishing her husband was somewhere or someone else. Or she wins her way in disagreements by refusing everything from laundry to lovemaking.

Sometimes a wife puts a personal stamp on the ever popular, "Do it yourself" method. If her husband asks her to do something she says, "Do it yourself." In Genesis 18.6 Abraham said to Sarah, "Make ready quickly three measures of fine meal, knead it, and make cakes." Can you imagine Sarah telling Abraham, "Do it yourself"? It would have been totally out of character for her, for "Sarah obeyed Abraham, calling him Lord."

"Holy women of old," such as Sarah, "adorned" themselves with the apparel of a "meek and quiet spirit...being in subjection to their own husbands." Their humility enhanced their beauty (1 Pet 3.3–6). A haughty attitude would have degraded both Sarah and Abraham.

These verses don't tell husbands to make their wives be in sub-jection. The women who "hoped in God," "adorned themselves" with subjection. Again, in Colossians 3.18 and Ephesians 5.22, it's the wife's responsibility to respect her husband, unlike the bumper sticker that published a wife's attitude toward hers: "All husbands are idiots and mine is king." Think her husband ever borrowed her car?

If the husband slights his responsibilities or is still learning how to lead, the wife's growth in submission is also stunted if she feels justified saying, "I'll do my part when he does his right." If she'll just hang in there while he gets the hang of it, both will benefit. God's word doesn't say to be in subjection when the husband is the perfect leader. The husband is responsible for his leadership role and the wife is to see to her subjection. If he gives up and goes along with unwise, selfish, or unreasonable demands to gain his wife's favor, he risks eventually losing her respect and his own self-respect as well.

First Peter 3.1–2 teaches the wife to be in subjection to her husband even when he isn't a Christian. Her attitude of respect toward him and her chaste behavior can win him to the word. Letting him see that her being a Christian doesn't cause her to look down on him, but rather helps her look up to his position as husband is more effective than continually whopping him with the word. Acts 5.29 is the qualifier if a wife's unbelieving husband wants her to go against Scripture: "We must obey God rather than men."

Likewise

First Peter 3.7 teaches some "likewise" lessons to husbands. "Likewise," husbands are to "dwell with them with understanding, giving honor to the wife. …Being heirs together of the grace of life, that your prayers be not hindered" (NKJV). If the husband disregards his wife's feelings, or disrespects her, his prayers will be "hindered." If she is haughty or rebellious, he must guard against being bitter (see also Col 3.19).

Some husbands take an unreasonable approach to subjection saying, "If I let her have a say in anything she might take over." Others make subjection difficult by acting like overbearing bullies. The laid-back, "Let George do it" type lets his responsibilities slide over onto his wife's shoulders. If she finds this comfortable, or encourages it with an "Anything you can do I can do better" attitude, she subverts the blessings of subjection she might have enjoyed. The loving wife wants to complete, not compete.

First Peter 3.1–7 brings husbands and wives back to togetherness. They have an attitude of honor toward each other. God didn't design a marriage of two competing individuals, fighting his plan and each other, but of a loving, respectful, insightful, devoted husband and wife who are "joint heirs of the grace of life."

"And Not Evil"

Next, to "She doeth him good" here in Proverbs 31.12, the inspired writer adds the negative "and not evil." A wife has an awesome influence on her husband for "good" or "evil." Her opportunity for physical and emotional closeness and unlimited use of her womanly attributes makes her husband vulnerable to her attitudes, viewpoints, and desires.

For example, 1 Kings 11.3 states that among all the wives, princesses, and concubines Solomon had, "his wives turned away his heart after other gods." He built "high places" for "all his foreign wives, who burnt incense and sacrificed unto their gods." They helped deplete his spiritual strength and topple his physical kingdom.

"But," some say, "those were ungodly women." But how godly are we? Do we "seek first the kingdom of God and his righteousness " and encourage our husbands to do so? Or do we "turn away his heart" after the gods of materialism, pleasure, and self? (Matt 6.33)

Solomon committed spiritual suicide by marrying ungodly, idolatrous women whose influences overpowered even his renowned wisdom. In contrast, the worthy woman did her husband good "all the days of her life." Realizing our effect on our husband's life lifts our study of the worthy woman out of the casual category and urges us on in our pursuit of excellence.

"All the Days of Her Life"

"Grow old along with me, the best is yet to be." To the sentiment of Robert Browning many older husbands and wives add an experienced "Amen" and countless young married couples a hearty "I hope so." A worthy woman helps ensure the best yet years as she does her husband "good," not only as a young bride, but later when her youthful brightness fades.

Sarah shines down through the ages as an example of one of beauty of face and faith who did her husband good all the days of her life. The tribute to her in Hebrews 11 shows that her inner adornment became more beautiful, even as she outwardly aged.

She honored her husband until her death when "Abraham came to mourn for Sarah, and to weep for her" (Gen 23.2).

Sarah was not as Solomon's wives who "turned away his heart when he was old."

> "The wisest of the wise
> Listen to pretty lies,
> And love to hear them told.
> Doubt not that Solomon
> Listened to many a one,
> Some in his youth and more when
> He grew old."
>
> —Walter Landor

Husbands and wives who listen to God's truths rather than "pretty lies" from any source will enjoy a wonderful oneness that even Solomon craved all the days of their lives (Ecc 7.28).

A precious heritage from parents to their children is letting them see in them a loving, lasting relationship as God designed it. It also brings joy to others to see husbands and wives growing old together, allowing both happiness and heartaches to meld their oneness, treating their marriage vows as a clasp of love rather than a padlock to be picked when there are challenges.

It heartens fellow worshippers to look over the assembly and see the "silver-haired" heads worshipping their Creator, knowing He faithfully strengthened and blessed them through life, and by their faithfulness encouraging others to enjoy a lifetime of service to Him. "The silver-haired head is a crown of glory, if it is found in the way of righteousness" (Prov 16.31 NKJV).

Sitting ahead of us, one Sunday morning, a 91-year-old gentleman reached over and patted his wife's arm. She took his hand, and Charlie and Billie sat worshipping together. "Enjoy life with the woman whom you love all the days of your fleeting life which He has given to you under the sun; for this is your reward in life and in your toil in which you have labored under the sun" (Ecc 9.9 NASU).

Questions

1. How do we know man's need for a help meet is by divine design?

2. What does "that which is good" include? (Tit 2.3–5)

3. From Titus 2.2–5 who should be soberminded?

4. How does "being in subjection" benefit both husband and wife?

5. How can not doing the things listed in Titus 2.4–5 blaspheme God's word?"

Strength Training

Isometrics anyone? It's easy to let your marriage slip into I-sometrics. One person tensing against the other. Everything centered around self: "I," "Me." Exercise can change "Me" to "We."

Exercise 1. Read James 3.13–18. What is the source of "self-seeking"? What are the results?

Exercise 2. This week meditate on these verses and use them to strengthen your relationship with each other.

Exercise 3. Meditate on Isaiah 40.29–31 and gain strength for your struggles.

Worthy Woman
Sarah

The Lord's instructions to Abram involved and affected Sarai. They obediently left kin and culture and, with their entourage of people, possessions, donkeys, goats, and sheep, set out for the land of Canaan. Throughout the slow, dusty 600-mile journey to Shechem, she did not look back with regret nor ahead with fear, but steadfastly followed her husband. Sarai was barren of child, but a great faith was growing within her as she shared in the excitement and mystery of God's promises to Abram.

God again appeared to Abram, changed his name to Abraham, meaning "A father of many nations," and further explained and extended His promises to him. God then changed Sarai's name to Sarah, saying, "And I will bless her and also give you a son by her, and she shall be a mother of nations..."

When Abraham was "advanced in age" the Lord again appeared to him with a visit from three men, as he sat in his tent door beneath the oaks of Mamre. As Sarah quickly kneaded three measures of fine meal for the messengers, she could not have imagined the measure of their message.

Then, standing behind Abraham in the tent door, she overheard the startling words: "Sarah, your wife, shall have a son." Sarah, well past the age of child-bearing, laughed and questioned within herself. The Lord reproved Sarah to Abraham saying, "Is anything too hard for the Lord?" At the "set time" Sarah conceived and bore Abraham a son "in his old age." After the birth of Isaac, Sarah's life continued to be a fascinating adventure of faith.

Sarah's beauty was praised by men and was such Abraham feared men might kill for. God praised Sarah's inner beauty; her holiness, trust in God, and inner adornment of honor and submission to her husband in 1 Peter 3.5–6, and her faith in Hebrews 11. Her weaknesses along life's way showed she was human, trying to live by faith on their journey to the "city" God has prepared.

Sarah honored her honorable husband Abraham throughout her life of 127 years. He honored her in life and in death as he "came to mourn for Sarah and to weep for her." Abraham, called a "mighty prince" by the sons of Heth who deeded him the field of Machpelah for Sarah's burial, now buried his princess, the meaning of the word "Sarah."

Abraham and Sarah's faith in God traveled with them all the way from Ur of the Chaldeans through the pages of the New Testament where God honors their great faith: "By faith Abraham…" "by faith… Sarah herself…" (Gen 12–2; Acts 7.1–4; Heb 11.8–19).

The worthy woman Sarah did "her husband good all the days of her life," as did the worthy woman of Proverbs 31.12. When we live lives of faith, and "do good," we can be as Sarah's daughters (1 Pet 3.6 NKJV).

Facets
Together

Together
they tend their garden of lifetime,
choosing seed carefully-sowing,
knowing, "You reap what you sow."

Thankful for good soil, and strength for the tending.
Thinking of bounty and reward to come.
Faith, love, and trust, each rooting deeply.
Weeding though weary, under rain and hot sun.

Loving attention
to God given seedlings.
Feeding, pruning,
watching them grow.

Cultivating kindness on through the dry spells.
Dead-heading faults to encourage the blooms.
Each doing their part—ever rejoicing,
though dark weather looms.

Often they labor,
tilling for others,
hearts looking heavenward,
two bent as one.

Now resting more often
in the last of life's seasons,
drenched in contentment,
the hardest work done.

Harvest is near now.
Through storm clouds and rainbows,
hearts and hands clasped in marriage,
still warmly entwined.

Together
they watch through the rose-grey sunset.
Two souls watching closely
for each other's passing,
Through God's garden gate.

Darlene Craig – 2008

FOUR

She seeketh wool and flax
And worketh willingly with her hands.
She is like the merchant-ships;
She bringeth her bread from afar.

Verse 13 reveals an underlying element that lights up every area of the worthy woman's life. It shines the ideal approach the ideal woman activates on all she is and does.

But first, verse 13 shows this woman of action in action. "She seeketh wool and flax...." She searches out and gathers in raw materials for garments and furnishings. "The herbs of the mountains are gathered in. The lambs are for their clothing, and the goats for the price of the field" (Prov 27.25–26).

Goat's hair, specified for use in the tabernacle (Exod 35.6, 23, 26), was considered the softest wool. The Angora goat provides long, silky mohair wool. A cashmere sweater helps you appreciate the soft, wool undercoat of the Cashmere goat. And when with your little granddaughter, you pat the soft hair on her baby goat's tummy, surely it is the softest of all.

Though the wool of goats and camels was also used, sheep were more common to most areas in Bible times. Women today enjoy working with wool such as the soft wool of the Merino, Blue-faced Leicester, and the Shetland sheep. Psalm 147.16 shows the original source of wool and pictures for us its color and fluffiness: "He giveth snow like wool."

Wool and flax rated high on the worthy woman's shopping list. Flax grows from one to four feet tall, has small leaves, tiny blue flowers, and ancient roots. Exodus 9.31 references it as far back as 1325 BC. The hail struck it down when "the flax was in bloom." Rahab saved two spies' lives when she "hid them with the stalks of flax, which she had laid in order upon the roof" (Josh 2.6).

Flax can be spun into items ranging from coarse rope and fishing nets to the fine linen worn by the worthy woman. Ezekiel 27.7 describes the fine linen sails of the ships of Tyre. Joseph of Arimathea wrapped the body of Jesus in linen before he laid it in his own new tomb (Matt 27.57–60). (See also chs 8–9)

Cultural Exchange

Wouldn't it be enlightening to go back in time with the women of old as they sought wool and flax and worked with it from flock and field to finish? And wouldn't it be fascinating to transport them to a modern fabric shop and watch their eyes light up at the rainbow rows of fabric already woven and ready for the eager seamstress? The process and quality of their sturdy handmade goods would impress us, while the variety and convenience of ready-made might seem a mirage to those whose gathered wool waited to be washed, dried, dyed, and carded.

The minds of those who took the trip to today while their flax dried would be spinning as they hurried home to pound, comb, and spin it into linen thread. A common thread that weaves womanly hearts together through time is the centuries of work done with willing hearts and hands.

The Four Ws

Verse 13 shows the worthy woman at work. Work demonstrates character performing purposeful action. She energetically worked for desired results. Proverbs 6.6–8 gives the ant as an example of industry. The ant is an energetic little self-starter working toward a goal. In contrast, the sluggard described in Proverbs 13.4 has desires but no desire to work. The worthy woman had both. She worked "willingly."

We are all familiar with the Three Rs and consider them essential to a good education. In Proverbs 31.10–31 I have found four Ws that are essential to the life of a Worthy Woman. They are Worthy Woman Worketh Willingly. These four Ws carry a mighty message.

Verses 10–12 showed the significance of the first two Ws: Worthy Woman. Then the first part of verse 13 added the third W: Worketh. Now, verse 13 reveals the fourth W: Willingly. Willingly fills out the four Ws formula. A Worthy Woman Works Willingly.

Willingly is the "light up your life" part. The NASB and the NASU use "in delight" in verse 13. The worthy woman delights in her work. She epitomizes the fourth W—Willingly. Her joyful inner action illuminates her outer action. Delight delivers.

As I sit attempting to define "in delight," seven yellow-brown ducklings demonstrate it for me. Mama Mallard leads her energetic little fuzz balls down the tiny creek. They scramble over the slippery stones, tug at wet grass roots, and bob for bugs. All fall in, bob back up, and splash forward. I feel privileged to view this delightful scene, and their enthusiasm for their job boosts mine.

Delight in our work revs up the engines regardless of the horsepower. We mourn our physical handicaps yet limit ourselves with negative attitudes, even in the dailies. For example, does the beat of your heart slow to the humdrum at the thought of housework? Does homemaking seem like boxed-in boredom? Most efforts include monotony, even chosen hobbies.

Getting It Done

Search for the creative possibilities, whatever you're working on, and depression will change to determination. Dreary thoughts defeat energy and optimism. When the doldrums lurk to capture your mind, fight them with "delight'. Delight and dread can't occupy your mind at the same time. Help your "willingly" win.

Some rely on a fifth and futile W: Wish. The worthy woman doesn't daydream her potential away or leave her life to "lady luck." She works at being the best she can be.

Optimism without elbow grease won't get the work done, but optimism evicts inertia. It helps you buzz through your work, enjoying the process as well as the results. Sometimes fast and frazzled fits your schedule, but when possible, make time to enjoy de-cluttering the family room and stirring the cookie batter. Sniff the sweetness of the berries as you freeze them for winter. Feel good about the freshly filed paperwork. Think about the wearers as you match their socks. Focus on their good qualities and how to direct their feet.

Now if your eager attitude toward your work causes you to spend extra time at it, especially leisure time, some might think you're a workaholic. Nervous, nit-picky work that's forced with little regard for health or the needs of others might merit the label, but there is no need to apologize for the joy of productive activity.

Those who take time, strength, and energy for extra effort are sometimes thought of as perfectionists. Instead, maybe they are appreciationists. Many who have experienced times of little show appreciation for their blessings by taking care of them. Willing stewardship.

The Whistle in Your Work

"Willingly" is the whistle in your work. Remember the catchy song from Snow White and the Seven Dwarfs that makes you want to "whistle while you work"? Chants have cheered work and play through the ages. Workers matched the rhythm of their field work to the rhythm of song. Evangeline helps us hear the "songs of the maidens" as they spun flax. Songs such as "To The Work" energize hearts and inspire Christians on to willing work. When a joyful homemaker sings or hums her "delight" in her work, the work hums along too.

Want to really wind up the willing? Colossians 3.17 adds a dynamic dimension to "delight." It puts in simple words a profound approach for work of every sort. "And whatsoever you do, do it heartily, as to the Lord and not to men." "As to the Lord" gives purpose and dignity to work, even work that you might think drudgery, or work done for someone who demeans you. "As to the

Lord" joys your perspective, gladdens your heart with gratitude, and helps you work "willingly," or "in delight."

Delight can be contagious. During a trip to Anchorage, Alaska, my husband and I took a short dog sled ride. As the go-getter Alaskan huskies yipped and jumped at their harnesses in anticipation, then enthusiastically swooshed our sled over the snow, those willing workers almost made me want to put my head in the harness with them.

Willing Hearts and Hands

Exodus 35.4–36.7 shows what a powerful combination willing hearts and hands can make. Moses spoke the words of Jehovah to the children of Israel and "whosoever" was "of a willing heart" went to work for the building of the tabernacle:

> Then came everyone whose heart stirred him up. And everyone whom his spirit made willing. ...And they came, both men and women, as many as were willing-hearted. ...And all the women that were wise-hearted did spin with their hands, and brought that which they had spun...the blue, and the purple, and the scarlet, and the fine linen. And all the women whose hearts stirred with wisdom spun yarn of goat's hair.

The wisdom and whirring in their hearts caused them to willingly spin for the work. They "brought a free-will offering unto Jehovah; every man and woman, whose heart made them willing...." Their "stirred" hearts caused them to bring "much more than enough. ...So the people were restrained from bringing. For the stuff was sufficient for all the work...and too much."

Think of the joy generated and the work accomplished by these willing-hearted people. These verses vibrate with their enthusiasm. Wise and willing hearts will cause us to use our time, talents, energies, resources, and modern equipment for our families, and the Lord's work. (Chapter 7 shows willing hearts and hands stretching and reaching out to others.)

Merchant Ships

Next, in verse 14, we see the four Ws at work: "She is like the merchant ships, She bringeth her bread from afar."

A merchant ship sets out to sea. Muscles ripple, oars glint in the sun, sails wave in the wind moving the sturdy sea going vessel over the majestic deep. Within are "they that go down to the sea in ships, that do business in great waters" (Psa 107.23). The shipmaster, mariners, and merchants are a robust blend of shrewdness, daring, and "knowledge of the sea." Salt and excitement mingle in the air as "those who gain their living by sea" face the challenge of the deep in anticipation of the challenge of the marketplace.

Let's imagine ourselves aboard ship and join them in admiring their wares and picturing the price the cargo will bring in faraway ports. Perhaps the ship laden with silver, iron, tin, gold, and ivory comes from Tarshish. Emeralds and rubies sparkle amid fine linen, purple embroidered work, and coral on the Syrian ship. A ship from Judah carries wheat, minnith, pannag, honey, oil, and balm. The smell of rare spices draws us to the cargo from Raamah and Shebah to marvel at the glittering gold and other precious stones. Ship merchants mentally outsmart the market merchants and reload their ships with the treasures they dream of acquiring from distant isles.

Phoenicia, a narrow coastal region famous for abundance and ability, set many ships to sea. Ezekiel 27 shows the scope of Phoenicia's sea operations and describes Tyre's superb location which contributed to the area's wealth. "O thou that dwellest at the entry of the sea. …Thy borders are in the heart of the seas." Verses 4–7 pay tribute to the ship builder's craftsmanship, and verse 8 to the oarsmen and pilots. The Lebanon range behind its seaports provided "cedars from Lebanon" and "timber of fir" furthering Phoenicia's reputation as "the merchants of the peoples unto many isles."

The Ancient Market

Just as the seamen sailed to the distant ports to buy and barter, the worthy woman moves out from her home base to increase the food and textile supply for her household. Just as the shipmaster chose the right port at the right time, she knows the offerings of the marketplace. She goes to market early while the temperature is low and the carts, booths, and ground displays are piled high with fruits, vegetables, spices, baskets, and baked goods. Maidens carry her barter of home-grown produce and handmade garments while she examines seasonal specialties.

The smell of bread baking in the village ovens welcomes the locals and travelers arriving through the city gates, donkeys and oxen through the larger ones, and scruffy dogs sniffing their way through the narrow streets and alleys. Hooves, handcarts, and colorfully clad people provide a steady clatter-chatter as friends and merchants swap greetings and goods. Streets, stalls, and booths are abuzz as beneath colorful head pieces, the alert eyes of the local, caravan, and sea merchants assess the barter and heartily haggle over prices.

She manages the hustle-bustle atmosphere of the local marketplace with the strength and presence of the stalwart merchant ships as she selects and trades wares with the enterprising eye of a sea merchant.

The worthy woman trades the products of willing hands for spices, honey, or purple, as farm women of later years traded butter and eggs for a neighbor's lettuce, corn, or cotton. The local vocal news announces a camel caravan approaching the city. Genesis 37.25–28 gives an example of caravan merchandising when Joseph's brothers sold him to the Ishmaelite merchants.

Modern Markets

Today shopping opportunities come in many forms, determined by season and location. In Oregon's Willamette Valley we have neighborhood markets, supermarkets, street markets, one stops, roadside stands boasting ripe-picked produce, acres of luscious fruits, and vegetables, both u-pick and been picked. Parents' and children's muddy knees and berry stained fingers testify to their help in the picking. Home gardens prompt swapping and sharing. One gardener's prolific zucchini plant is a friend or fellow gardener's zucchini bread.

We once lived near Seattle's Pike Place Market. This flower-splashed farmer's market boasts block-long rows of wooden tables piled high with farm-fresh produce in a kaleidoscope of country garden colors. The edible displays include lettuces, juicy berries and tomatoes, crackly heads of cabbage, red, green, and yellow peppers, apples, plums, melon, and green onions so fresh you expect to see garden soil on the hand that returns your change. The Puget Sound breeze cooperates by leaving just enough fresh fish smell in the air to lure you to large, glass-covered cases in search of your favorite Northwest seafood where lively fishmongers will toss the fish to you. Pastas, breads, and cheeses join in the fun calling, "Take me home too."

Seasonal shopping played a part in ancient markets as it does today. Today's shopper appreciates modern marketing and shipping that makes it possible to slurp a sun-soaked Florida orange in the rainy northwest while southerners sample the cool, crisp climate packaged in a shiny, red-skinned Oregon apple.

Shopping Day Blues

America's shopping opportunities are as varied as its people and places, but feeding a family is still a challenge. Individual plight worsened by the current economy can make finding the "delight" in the reality difficult. For some, having a car, gas, cash, or credit seems a dream. Many clip coupons, stretch food stamps, and join those waiting for sales. They gaze at the exotic offerings of the grocery aisles, then sigh back to "How many ways can I fix a sack of potatoes, a dozen eggs, and should I splurge on a chunk of cheese?" Shredded potatoes with some eggs and minced onions mixed in and a sprinkle of cheese on top would be a gourmet meal for many. Mom dresses up her budget blues with a willing attitude as she spruces up the day old bread as a fancy French toast treat.

Even in easier times it can strain the brain and budget to plan, pick out, and purchase food for a family. Some days you drag yourself to the store, trudge up and down the aisles, dump the food into the cart, go back home, push it into the fridge or cupboards, pull it back out, and cook away at it until it's gone, dreading doing it all over again.

On those days don't shop alone. Along with your list, ads, and coupons, take your Four Ws mindset and a thankful heart to help push the cart through your modern market. Delight in the fresh fruits and vegetables, sanitary meat and fish displays, shiny packages, and sparkling jars and bottles all arranged for your air-conditioned convenience, then mentally transport yourself to the ancient market of the worthy woman's day where produce often wilted in the hot, humid air, buzzed by flies and brushed by animals. Figs, olives, and spices heated up while you haggled with the merchants before your steamy walk home to store your purchases in the simple pottery containers.

Back at your modern market, weigh your fresh, set-priced produce on the electronic scale, pay at the computerized checkout, drive home in your comfortable vehicle, put your groceries in your cold refrigerator, freezer, or handy cupboard, then sit down, put your feet up, and count your blessings.

Appreciating our "daily bread" helps us be truly thankful as we bow our heads before each meal and in between. Ephesians 5.20 reminds, "Giving thanks always for all things in the name of our Lord Jesus Christ to God, even the Father," whether we shop the supermarket, farmer's market, or the neighborhood grocery.

Smorgasbord

"She bringeth her bread from afar." In Proverbs 31.14 "bread" refers to food in general as in Genesis 3.19; "In the sweat of your face you shall eat bread" (NKJV). Other scriptures show some of the foods grown and apt to be available in the marketplace. Moses described Canaan as "a land of wheat and barley, and vines, and fig trees, and pomegranates; a land of olive trees, and honey" (Deut 8.7–8). Jacob's sons took "balm…honey, spicery, and myrrh, nuts and almonds" back to Egypt with them (Gen 43.11). During their wilderness wanderings the children of Israel complained they weren't getting the fish, cucumbers, leeks, onions, garlic, and melons they ate in Egypt (Num 11.5).

Among Abigail's peace-offerings to David were loaves, parched corn, dressed sheep, raisins, and cakes of figs (1 Sam 25.18). Shobi and Machir brought David and his people food such as wheat, barley, beans, lentils, honey, butter, and cheese (2 Sam 17.29). Job thought the white of an egg tasteless, and salt a flavor saver (Job 6.6). The bread recipe ingredients in Ezekiel 49 were wheat, barley, beans, lentils, millet, and spelt.

Bread Basket

The smell of baking bread wafts down through the ages from the first simple stone oven over goat hair tents and flat village roof tops into our sleek twenty-first century kitchens. Women of earlier ages often baked wheat or barley bread, usually leavened, then set it to rise in wooden kneading bowls (Exod 8.3).

When the Israelites hurriedly left Egypt they "took their dough before it was leavened, having their kneading bowls bound up in their clothes on their shoulders" (Exod 12.34). Moses told the Israelites if they obeyed God, "Blessed shall be your baskets and your kneading bowl." If they did not obey, "Cursed shall be your basket and your kneading bowl" (Deut 28.5, 17 NKJV).

Their hands formed the daily bread, or cakes, in flat seven to ten-inch rounds, from crispy thin to an inch thick. Sometimes they baked it by placing the dough on hot stones and turning it when half done, as we turn pancakes on a griddle. God describes Ephraim as a "cake not turned." They were spiritually soggy and not yet pleasing to God. (Hos 7.8)

An angel used hot stone cooking to help convince Elijah to eat. "And he looked and, behold, there was at his head a cake baked on the coals, and a cruse of water" (1 Kgs 19.4–6; footnote: "Hot stones."). Some made their ovens by inverting a clay bowl over hot stones. Bread baked under the bowl while they piled hot ashes over the top. Dry thorns made quick start kindling for the sometimes gritty dough. (Psa 58.9)

Today breads ranging from white to near black, with or without seeds, nuts, fruits, vegetables, cheese, oils, preservatives, coloring ,and calories, in loaf form or pre-sliced, snazzily wrapped, or in brown paper sacks pack store shelves. Bread, pizza, and pie dough come mixed, frozen, and ready to bake. Rolls and biscuits wait, tucked in cozy cans ready to be tapped out. Ancient day bakers might not recognize some of the pale, puffed up breads that are more like dessert than the hearty chunks that shepherds carried in their leather belts or bags or that sustained the farmer as he worked the rocky hillside vineyards.

Bread making, once nearly a lost art, is again on the rise. Stressful times seem to create a craving for back to basics comfort food. Kneading dough can be therapeutic for both muscles and psyche and bread-making machines and mixers with dough hooks help if your strength doesn't match your baking ambition.

Homemade biscuits are a quick-bread solution, either the mix and roll out or the stir and pat type. Add-ins such as fruit, nuts, grated cheese, beaten egg, wheat germ, dry powdered milk, and spices make a heartier scone-like version. Over the years I made jillions of them as a simple way to fix our family something special that fit my strength and budget.

Recently a granddaughter carefully cut out her biscuit dough choosing heart and doll shapes. Her brothers joined in, filling their pan with tree and deer shapes in quick, boyish, "When do we eat 'em?" style. Shortcuts are welcome time and energy savers, but homemade can be more fun than routinely opening a box of Misquick.

It's also fun to sit engulfed in giggles descending from the loft above where a whirl of grandgirls invent imaginative menus and fix pretend food to bring down to grandpa and grandma.

As we think ahead to the miles of meals, let's mentally slip back into the worthy woman's sandals, walk the marketplace of her culture, grind at her hand mill, and bake on her clay oven as we stoke our willing hearts, and use our hands, energy, and resources to plan, purchase, and prepare "bread" to satisfy the needs and pleasures of our household.

Questions

1. What is the base word for each of the Four **W**s?

2. How does the last **W** affect the things a woman does for her family and others?

3. Why does Colossians 3.17 change our perspective on work?

4. How is the worthy woman "like the merchant ships" (Prov 31.14)?

5. What caused Tyres markets of wisdom and splendor to crash in the "heart of the seas" (Ezek 28.1–8)?

Strength Training

1. Time for Attitude Aerobics? We all have times when our willing attitude goes into hiding. Share ideas to get it to say "Yoo hoo, I'm back."

2. Serve up some time, energy, or money saving ideas for grocery shopping, meals, or treats for your family. I like to make chicken soup and pasta sauce at the same time. Chop the onions, garlic, celery, etc. for both, put some of the broth in the sauce before you freeze the extra broth into cubes or containers. Reserve some cooked chicken for salads or sandwiches, and some cooked pasta sauce meat for future tacos, omelets, etc. (I fry the yucky chicken livers for my husband.) You can make lentil soup at the same time with the meat, broth, and veggies and start a salad while you have stuff out. You end up with many meals or possibilities with one main mess.

Here is an experiment that works for me. My family likes home whipped cream. I whip a large carton near stiff, with powdered sugar (doesn't get watery), then freeze small puffs of the leftover in a mini-muffin tin ready to pop one or more on a cup of hot chocolate, fruit pancakes, a dessert, into an almost healthy smoothie, or to cream up a mocha.

Worthy Woman
Dorcas

Joppa, a seaport town on a raised ledge above a rocky part of the Mediterranean coast, was the setting for an unusual drama. The time was about AD 32. Acts 9.36–43 presents the story. It begins with a leading character, Tabitha, whose name was translated Dorcas. Dorcas, who was "full of good works and almsdeeds which she did" became sick and died. The grieving women lovingly washed her and "laid her in an upper room."

The disciples sent two men to Lydda, about nine miles north, to urge Peter to "Delay not to come." When Peter came they took him to the upper floor. There he was audience to a unique fashion show. The widows displayed and modeled the garments Dorcas made for them. Tears of love and gratitude spattered their coats and tunics as they told him all she had done "while she was with them."

He sent them out, then kneeled and prayed. Then he looked at the body and said, "Tabitha, arise." She opened her eyes, saw Peter, and sat up. Peter now gave his hand to the one whose hands had willingly worked to help others, and "raised her up."

Next he called the saints and widows and "presented her alive." Imagine the joy and excitement of those in Joppa who were audience to this inspiring scene and the many who believed on the Lord when they heard about it.

Alive again, did Dorcas take wool and flax in her hands and continue her work? Was she wealthy, or had her servant heart sacrificed to do this work? Was her house among those above the harbor where she saw fishermen's widows weeping, as the fishing vessels that carried their husbands out to sea washed in without them? Were those she helped "widows indeed" described in 1 Timothy 5.5–10 as "having diligently followed every good work"? Were they younger widows with children? Perhaps Dorcas was widowed.

There are many details we want to know about Dorcas. She didn't have a speaking part, but her actions told the woman she was. Dorcas was a real woman of New Testament times who lived out the example of the ideal woman of Proverbs 31, as she sought wool and flax for fabric and worked willingly with her hands to help others.

Facets
Dollar Store Delight

Swaying slightly to the Dollar Store's in-store music, the young woman glided past me, whirled her cart around to the next aisle, tossed in a pack of yellow sponges, and stood cheerfully studying the shelf of cleaning supplies. Then she swooped up a bottle of liquid cleaner and a toilet bowl brush and tossed them in her cart.

Her "Isn't this fun?" smile when she caught me watching, brightened her faded cotton dress as she twirled toward the plastic buckets. A "Woe is me" woman dressed in designer clothing and shopping for toiletries in an upscale market wouldn't have seemed nearly so delightful.

FIVE

She riseth also while it is yet night:
And giveth food to her household,
And their task to her maidens.
She considereth a field and buyeth it;
With the fruit of her hands she planteth
A vineyard.

After reading the original *A Worthy Woman*, a young woman wrote me a letter that underscored the value of studying Proverbs 31.10–31, including the housework parts. Her mom left her dad and the kids when she was a pre-teen, and the oldest. So at the age when mom might have taught her to cook, clean, and get along in a family setting, a lot of things were dumped on her. They didn't have money for extra help, and their lifestyle didn't include a Titus 2 support system.

When she got married and had kids, she wished for help. Now she was using the book for a daily Bible study, to reorganize her life and with practical things. Her touching letter reminds that each woman's needs are different. Help in an area that seems simple to one is sought after by another. God's word includes taking care of our homes and family, and Titus 2 tells the older women to get the word out.

Up and at 'Em Attitude

What can we learn from the worthy woman's daily routine to help us with our own? "Willingly" wakes her up. "She riseth also while it is yet night" (Prov 31.15). She is like stored sunlight as God's gift of sleep relaxes and re-energizes her mind and body. Then she is up before the sun releasing her energies in a rainbow of activities.

For many the biggest chore of all is getting out of bed. Beds of her times were often portable pallets that could be rolled up to make space in a nomad's tent or the small house of the average family. The wealthier had cots, couches, or beds, sometimes canopied with tapestries or curtains. Modern manufacturers seem to scheme to make getting up harder with comfort choices from replicas of Grandma's featherbed to dial-a-soft, switch-a-position, or conform-to-your-form.

Some mornings you need an eject button. That fifth piece of pizza spent the night chastising you, or you were up with a newborn or sick children. Perhaps pain poked you awake at 3:00 AM or the phone woke you, and the caller's sad message echoed in your heart all night long. Or, the neighbor's barking dog made you forget your love for animals, not to mention "love your neighbor."

The morning after a sleepless night finds you in a muddling through mood. Mind and body have the right to complain if they are regularly cheated out of rest. But when healthy people get enough sleep and still have to be blasted out of bed due to a time wasting battle with reality, they are in for a life of vim-dimming frustration.

True, sleep needs vary, depending on individual make-up, health, stress, activity, and schedules. My husband claims I wake the birds up, though these days I often relate to the words of Jim Berryman who says "I get up early, but wake up late."

After our class on this verse one young wife who was "just not a morning person," jumped out of bed and cheerfully fixed breakfast. Her surprised husband said, "Well, what got you up?" She smiled mysteriously and said, "I just felt like it." She's right. Once we make our minds up the body usually follows and we do "just feel like it."

AM Appetites

She "giveth food to her household." "And you shall have goats' milk enough for your food, for the food of your household, and the nourishment of your maidens" (Prov 27.27; Psa 123.2 NKJV).

Planning ahead helps make breakfast happen. Mix dry ingredients the night before for muffins, biscuits, or pancakes. Stir up pancake batter, but save the egg whites to fold in the next morning for tender cakes. Too early to face the eggy glop for french toast? Set thick, firm slices in the mixture, refrigerate overnight and they'll be pan ready in the morning.

Will breakfast be bolted and burped, or skipped completely as everyone rushes to meet deadlines? The possibility is enough to change "in delight" to the "why bothers." But hot cereal or peanut butter on toast is quick. Or set out the cold cereal. A pre-boiled egg makes a portable protein package, and you can swoosh lots of energy into a smoothie. Whatever suits your strength, budget and schedule.

Got a minute after breakfast to do something toward supper? Start a salad, a slow-cooker meal, or get something thawing. Of course, reality is that when nourishing do-aheads are most needed, there might not be time or strength to pre-do them.

When we had three babies under two and two children over, my preferred double-batch, freeze ahead approach often didn't make it from my mind to the freezer. Company meals were made from scratch rather than having the basics ready for guests, expected or otherwise. As the children grew, it took a big batch for the initial meal. Lifestyles, family size, and schedules vary, but when possible, head-starts help.

Some days all the ghosts of meals past parade before you, upstaged only by the haunting heaps of dirty dishes previously done. Visions of endless reruns of meal after meal almost wipes out your willing. But the Four Ws formula along with some creative and practical approaches can help make fun out of a fact of life.

Mealtime Madness

Dinnertime can be the biggest challenge when each brings the fatigue and frustrations of the day to the table. Add a phone call or two, a glass of spilled milk, a fussy baby, a sarcastic roll of the eyes, and chaos is the next course. In some households, McDonald's is as close to a "Happy Meal" as it gets. Tension can sabotage the potential for family refreshment and closeness. Dad comes to the table glum or growly, or mom feels irritable and unappreciated.

Most moms have had days when we were strained and drained, but still pushed to fix a big supper. Then, feeling cranky and put upon, we were upset to find ourselves spoiling the meal by picking at past behavior or present table manners—whatever seemed a target for our tension. Crushed spirits might have been saved by simpler fare and stomachs spared their curdled contents. "Pleasant words are as a honeycomb, sweet to the soul, and health to the bones" (Prov 16.24). Honeycomb words can make the whole dinner seem like dessert.

Have you ever had the "special dinner" glow dimmed by a grouchy waitress? No attempt at cheer could coax a smile except at tip time. Our mealtime manner also affects our families. "Better is a dinner of herbs where love is, than a fatted calf with hatred" (Prov 15.17). A simple meal served with love is more satisfying than haute cuisine with a hateful attitude.

Remember meals made memorable by the pleasant atmosphere even though the food was forgettable or occasions where the food impressed but anger oppressed? When the food thaws but the cook doesn't, stomachs begin to churn. "Better is a dry morsel and quietness, than a house full of feasting with strife" (Prov 17.1).

Turn the Tables

Prayer sets the table with praise and appreciation to God. Cheerful touches, including the children's colorful creations, and some "I care" cooking lift spirits when financial burdens are heavy. Some families have their daily Bible study during dinner. Others draw scriptures from a container for a roundtable discussion.

Fathers can help keep table talk positive so quarreling children don't change the menu to sarcasm soufflé or criticism casserole. When outbursts occurred I have resorted to an offender "fine" jar.

Knowing it might be used for liver if it gets full enough works with some children.

The family, including Dad and Mom, can each tell something about their day. All stay connected and learn from each other's interests, successes, and setbacks to empathize and support one another. Taking turns encourages the quieter child to speak while the talkative learn to listen. Willing help with clean up teaches cooperation, and refreshes Mom.

It's worthwhile to try to adjust activities such as part-time jobs, music, hobbies, sports, or whatever competes with togetherness, in order to eat together. Though sometimes hectic schedules may call for a "Get 'em out the door dinner," family bases are touched.

Helping Hands

The worthy woman's household is fed. Next, she gives "*their tasks to her maidens.*" Young maidens were often part of a household. "A little maiden…waited on Naaman's wife" (2 Kgs 5.2). A maiden helped rescue baby Moses (Exod 2.5–10). Their tasks would include those described in Proverbs 31 as well as drawing water (Gen 24.13), keeping sheep (Gen 29.9), and churning butter (Prov 30.33).

"But the worthy woman had 'maidens,'" we whine. What about our mechanical maidens? Electricity, stoves, refrigerators, freezers, mixers, blenders, washers, and dryers are some that would have lightened the load for women of her time. I lived without electricity from age five to 11 so I still appreciate that flip of the switch.

Once we zoomed through Kansas in our smooth riding, air-conditioned automobile alongside a remainder of the Oregon Trail. Out the right side of my mind's eye I could see a calico-clad pioneer woman, the covered wagon jostling her weary body as she held her crying infant, cooled only by the sight of the snow-covered mountains in the distance. Their simple supper waited to be warmed over a bonfire. As she faded from view, I contentedly patted the knee of my wagon master husband and felt blessed to be his twentieth century pioneer woman.

Still today, even for those who have modern appliances, family or friends who help regularly, or hire household help, it's a constant challenge to balance "tasks" with time and energy.

In earlier eras children also helped with household and outdoor chores. Children today learn their importance to a smooth running household when they help bring it about. Daughters who are pampered and picked up after might have a harder time accepting adult responsibilities. Sons also need to pitch in with a positive attitude toward work, an important part of manhood. Start young while it's play to do what mommy or daddy do, and before other activities compete for their time.

The husband's involved attitude supports a well-functioning family. How much he helps can depend on his schedule, his health, if his help is needed or wanted, and the thinking of both husband and wife. Be open-minded to the difference in men and women's viewpoints. You might think egg shells are hard on the garbage disposal, but he thinks that blade could handle the hide off an alligator.

Some wives take a business-like fifty-fifty or written contract approach to coerce cooperation. Others bully with, "You better do it or else." These methods don't harmonize with Bible teaching and do cause disharmony in the home. And acting like a mother figure who makes him do "his chores" can cause resentment and kill romance. Later verses show the worthy woman related to her household with wisdom and kindness.

Divide and Conquer

Does a late afternoon, "What's for supper, mom?" send you dashing to the freezer for a quick-thaw? Does it take a shivery, "Will someone puleeze bring me a towel?" from the shower to get a load in the dryer? Does clutter escape attention until someone trips over it answering the doorbell to an unexpected visitor? Are the closets full of hanger-only outfits, but nothing to wear for that looming appointment?

It might seem easy to only act as a reaction to deadlines or urgencies. Some claim to be laid back, but nearly get laid out by the stress they put themselves and others through when time's up.

Dividing big jobs into smaller ones simplifies. For example, spread out larger cleaning jobs rather than having a two-day house cleaning marathon that leaves your house in order, but you in shambles. Conquer the laundry so over-large loads won't overwhelm young helping hands or older tired ones. Hustle the smaller loads from dryer to drawers or hangers to decrease pressing.

Pretend you're moving. Sort out the don't fits, don't likes, and don't needs, and move out the extras. Donate them or give them to someone who needs them, perhaps along with something new. Organize and enjoy what's left. (Right now my closets and drawers are screaming at me, "Pretend you're moving.")

The worthy woman was organized. She started with herself, not in the popular "me first" sense, but in "shape me up first." The peace and order within herself pervaded her household.

Organizing comes easier for the self-starter than the "whenever" personality or the escape artist. A natural knack for planning and organization is an advantage, but working toward order is worth the effort for anyone. Planning helps make a happy, productive, many-faceted homemaker out of "just a housewife." Making a list helps.

Specialist

As the manager of your home, and with your husband's input, you are in the best position to know what works best for your family. You know its inner workings; its individual schedules, personalities, likes, dislikes, appointments, and disappointments. Some of these change regularly. When you creatively analyze your home and family and set up a satisfactory system, you become the specialist—a special person with a list.

You are the special person who puts your time, talent, energy, and creativity into a careful study of the unique necessities and possibilities for your home and family, puts your findings in list form, then works the list. 1 Thessalonians 4.11 encourages "that ye study to be quiet, and to do your own business, and to work with your hands...." Calmly studying your "own business" and diligently making a plan, whether in list form, calendar, notebook, software, or whatever suits you will show how time is spent, if goals are set and met, who or what needs extra attention, and what family priorities are.

Priorities

"But seek ye first his kingdom, and his righteousness, and all these things shall be added unto you" (Matt 6.33). This verse helps us live God centered, worshipful lives where worship assemblies and Bible study attendance don't slide down the list. Though unintentional, this can happen when we plan our lives too full.

Sometimes when young mothers begin to work outside their home, they feel they no longer have time to get themselves and the children to assemblies and Bible studies. "After all, we have to eat and wear clothes." This rationalization reverses the order of the above scripture for themselves and their family.

Upside down priorities and careening schedules can also weaken the husband's spiritual leadership in the family, his example to his family to "hunger and thirst after righteousness" (Matt 5.6), and diminish his own desire for spiritual service and growth.

Putting "Christ, who is our life..." (Col 3.4) first, simplifies our lives. When overwhelmed, ask, "What does He expect of me now, at this time of my life? What can I give up? What am I leaving out?" A "wise, redeeming the time" (Eph. 5.15,16) analysis reveals if our lives are empty and unproductive. Too full? Do we scramble the eggs then scramble through a day of Have Tos, Want Tos, and Shoulds? Do we know which is which?

Planning brings balance. It helps budget time as we would money; not overspending on pleasure while neglecting necessities such as food, or spending all on essentials with never a crumb for fun. An overall plan shows when the TV, phone, text messaging, video games, internet, reading, extra work, or hobbies support goals and when they defeat them. It prods the mentally lazy who never get around to an intellectual pursuit as well as those who are always in an academian fog that dims the down-to-earth dailies.

Plans help those who like to cook see when they spend so much time on delicious looking concoctions that their neglected homes become unappetizing. Those who enjoy keeping house keep it from becoming an oppressive taskmaster. The house still reflects care and creativity without the family feeling guilty of messing something up. It welcomes others without fearing it will reveal an imperfection or take time from improvement projects.

Once study, experiment, and family input results in a basic plan, you'll want to be flexible: when your four-year-old calls, "Mommy, can you come out and play?," your husband has an unexpected afternoon off and invites you for an outing, someone needs your sympathetic ear or offers some homegrown corn for the freezer.

A plan's purpose is to provide a base for a stable household, not act as a demanding warden. It saves our sanity when the Must Do's boggle our brain instead of coming through in single file. Completing a plan ensures satisfaction that procrastination puts off. It takes planning, interest, time, and work to turn a home into a snug, well-rounded retreat, but having a home the family wants to retreat to is a valuable part of a priority based lifestyle.

Value System

If a woman thinks she is "just a housewife," with unimportant, short-reaching, drudge duties, she will become a victim of her own value system. When she realizes her worth and the worth of her position of wife, mother, and homemaker, she becomes a willing worker who sets in motion a satisfactory system, knowing its far-reaching value to herself, her family, and those she reaches out to.

The Field

The worthy woman's attitude and organization enables her to take on other projects, for "she considereth a field and buyeth it."

The venture of verse 16 is a carefully thought out extension of their agricultural assets. This trustworthy woman studies the prospects before spending money or bartering goods. Her carefulness with her husband's earnings and those saved and earned through her own ingenuity helped make this purchase possible.

It wasn't a spurt of impulsive independence resulting in a real estate transaction.

Today there is also much to consider before a purchase such as quality, possibilities, risks, quantity needed, and the season. Will the venture devalue the family spiritually? Will it strain or reinforce relationships? How will it affect financial goals?

Buying a field in ancient times included many aspects besides price, such as land laws, condition and use of the field, preparation and upkeep, and results hoped for. Her decision included her husband's perspective and advice as they considered the field. Numbers 30.13 shows that the transaction would be carried out under his oversight since he had the right to undo it. "Every vow, and every binding oath to afflict the soul, her husband may establish it, or her husband may make it void."

The city elders also witnessed real estate transactions. Ruth 4 provides an example from the city gates of Bethlehem when Boaz "went up to the gate" concerning the land involving Naomi and "a close relative." He addressed the elders as "witnesses this day..." Ruth 4 gives more information concerning buying, selling, and inheritance that fits the pattern in Leviticus 25.25–26.

Because of the customs and laws regarding keeping land in a family the worthy woman's purchase would most likely be from a kinsman, and the property would be familiar to both husband and wife.

A Plot

In contrast to the worthy woman's lawful transaction, 1 Kings 21 reveals a wife's unscrupulous plot to gain a plot of land. Jezebel's husband Ahab, King of Samaria, offered to buy or trade for Naboth the Jezrelite's vineyard because it was close to the palace. Naboth responded, "Jehovah forbid it me, that I should give the inheritance of my fathers unto thee."

While Ahab pouted, Jezebel plotted to get Naboth's vineyard for him. "She wrote letters in Ahab's name and sealed them with his seal then sent the letters unto the elders and the nobles." The letters asked to have false witnesses set up against Naboth, saying he cursed God and the king, and then have him stoned.

After Naboth's death, Jezebel said to Ahab, "Arise, take possession of the vineyard of Naboth" because "Naboth is not alive, but dead." Jezebel's wicked ways eventually helped this evil husband and wife lose all of their possessions, whereas the worthy woman acted worthily and increased the family "gain."

The Vineyard

"With the fruit of her hands she planteth a vineyard." After buying the field she planted it with "the fruit of her hands"; perhaps vines bartered or bought with her earnings from earlier endeavors. Unlike our backyard gardens, it was probably outside the village since their homes were close together to protect from invaders and to be near a spring or well.

The land determined the crop she chose. The field was too hilly and rocky for grain, but workable for vine slips. First the rocks and stones had to be dug and cleared, then made into low walls topped by fencing from thorns to keep animals out. Isaiah 5.2 pictures the work necessary even in a "very fruitful hill" that "should bring forth grapes."

According to some scholars, since the Hebrew word for "planteth" was masculine, the husband or male servant did the actual planting. The worthy woman no doubt would have consulted her husband on a project that could involve his time and work. And, the owner being of "known in the gates" character, this vineyard wouldn't be covered with thorns and nettles and enclosed by a broken down wall like the field of the lazy man in Proverbs 24.30–32.

Meanwhile, the purchase completed and the work started, the worthy woman envisions the vineyard's potential: the first firm grapes, the sweet-tart reddish juice fresh from the winepress, the boiled down syrupy concentrate, the dried raisins for their household and to share with others. The work would be worthwhile.

Questions

1. What effect does a woman's AM attitude or actions have on her household's day?

2. How do planning and priorities relate?

3. What part does James 4.13–16 play in planning?

4. How does talking over financial situations benefit both husband and wife?

Strength Training

1. This week strengthen your morning spirit and transform your day with Psalm 118.24. (NKJV) "This is the day the Lord has made; we will rejoice and be glad in it ."

2. "This is the day…" Focus on today-not yesterday. "Forgetting those things which are behind…" (Phil 3.13). Learn from them and let them go. It's easy to obsess on "If only…"

3. "This is the day…." Focus on today-not tomorrow. "Be not therefore anxious for tomorrow…" (Matt 6.34). Don't let tomorrow's uncertainties steal today's joy or bring on the "I'll be happy when or if."

4. "Rejoice…." Celebrate this day and joyfully serve the Creator of it. Look to God (Col 3.1), then look for the good in this day—and the good you can do in it.

5. "Be glad in it…." Affirm with David: "The righteous shall be glad in Jehovah, and shall take refuge in him" (Psa 64.10). Gladly praise His power. "Light is sown for the righteous, and gladness for the upright in heart. Be glad in Jehovah, ye righteous; and give thanks to his holy memorial name" (Psa 97.11–12).

Worthy Woman
Rhoda

"Now about that time Herod the king put forth his hands to afflict certain of the church." Acts 12 relates that he killed James then, since that played politically popular with the Jews, seized Peter and put him in prison under the watch of four squads of guards. There, bound by two chains to two guards, Peter slept. Meanwhile, the church earnestly prayed for him.

Then "behold, an angel of the Lord stood by him, and a light shined in the cell." He told Peter to "Rise up quickly." His chains fell off, and the angel told him to get dressed and follow him. Peter followed him past two other guards through an iron gate which opened for them into the city, then to the first street, where the angel departed. Peter now knew for sure the Lord had sent His angel to deliver him from prison.

He went first "to the house of Mary, the mother of John… where many were gathered together and were praying," and knocked at the outer gate. While the others continued in fervent prayer, Rhoda, a young maiden, came to answer. When Rhoda recognized Peter's voice, she was joyful. He was alive. Their prayers had been answered. She was so excited she ran to tell the others—and left Peter standing at the gate.

"You are out of your mind." Did they discount her report because she was always excitable? Did they pray, and then as we often do, say "I can't believe it" when our prayer is answered? Did Peter think it was going to take the angel that opened the prison gates, and the city gate to open Mary's gate?

Rhoda "confidently affirmed" it was Peter at the gate. They said, "It is his angel." Peter kept knocking. When they finally opened the gate and saw Peter they "were amazed." Now, like Rhoda, they were excited. Peter quieted them, told what had happened, and left before Herod could find him.

Don't you just love Rhoda? Her enthusiasm. Her energy. Her belief. Her quickness to spread the joy. Her confidence in the truth, even when fellow Christians doubted. Rhoda, the servant girl who knew Peter's voice, is a happy example of truth from Galatians 3.27–28. Though we might think from Mary's evidently large house she was a woman of financial substance and Rhoda a simple servant girl, they were spiritual equals. "For as many of you as were baptized into Christ have put on Christ. There is neither Jew nor Greek, there is neither slave nor free, there is neither male nor female; for you are all one in Christ Jesus" (NKJV).

We don't know how old Rhoda was, except that she was old enough to be in charge of the outer gate during a time of danger to Christians. But don't you wonder about the rest of the life of this delightful young Rhoda, whose name meant Rose? Perhaps her excitability tempered with spiritual maturity, her joyous servant attitude, her faith, her energy and enthusiasm continued to blossom into the life of a worthy woman in full bloom.

Facets
Two In A Stew

I remember one attempt at thinking ahead that ended in a setback. I spent the evening simmering meat, scrubbing and chopping vegetables, a few at a time, resting in between additions, too weak to complete the process all at once, but spurred on by the hope of two days of nourishing lunches and suppers to count on, I kept at it until my huge kettle full of delicious smelling stew cooled on the breadboard.

Now, as mothers of young children know, one ill-timed push of a pull-out breadboard can disastrously demonstrate the law of gravity. The stew that was meant for six hungry stomachs was suddenly waxing the no-wax. Squelching my "What's the use?" I knelt with sinking spirits and wad of rags to sop up the soup, thinking my husband sure picked the right time to be out of town.

If my tears watered down the stew or added too much salt, our little cockapoo, who paddled into the puddle, didn't seem to mind as she lapped at it in tail-wagging wonder at my unexpected generosity.

Relating this stew saga stirs up the "I remembers" as all homemakers have similar frustrating experiences. But once we mop up the mess, and our emotions have simmered down, our willing attitude returns to help us surmount the setback.

SIX

She girdeth her loins with strength
And maketh strong her arms."
She perceiveth that her merchandise is profitable;
Her lamp goeth not out by night."
She layeth her hands to the distaff,
And her hands hold the spindle.

Just as the worthy woman belted her long, loose clothing around her waist for quicker movement, she "girded" or encircled herself with physical strength. She took action to take care of herself.

We can too. Many today take realistic measures toward good health. They don't wait to be coddled into taking care of themselves. They joyfully use their strong arms to serve their families and fellow man.

Others take their strength for granted until it is threatened or limited, then it would be fun to do what was a bore before. When a wife and mother even temporarily experiences the trauma of being unable to care for and live life fully with her family, her appreciation for strength quickens as her race becomes a slow walk.

Taking Action

Women experience different levels of health and strength during their lifetime. In my teens I swam in southern Oregon's Rogue River. Now, our Jacuzzi washes me downstream. Diet, exercise, environment, mental outlook, rest, stress, age, heredity, and happenings affect health. Many try to do the right things and still feel the wrong way through no fault of their own, perhaps an injury or accident.

Heredity also can seem unfair in the diseases it predisposes people to, but learning the potential prods you to take positive steps to lessen the likelihood or rein in the reality. Many exercise, manage their minds, eat healthy food, and search out the medical marketplace and alternative offerings to maximize physical strength.

The "latest word" on nutrition originated in God's word. The Mediterranean climate and lifestyle led to the basic diet of people of ancient times: Whole grains, nuts, legumes, olive oil, garlic, onions, grapes, figs, pomegranate, melon, fish, yogurt, herbs, and spices such as cinnamon and cumin were some of the foods they ate. Their natural diet came naturally as modern chemicals hadn't been added or the soil depleted.

A do-it-yourself study of nutrition and planning meals around nutritious foods is a worthwhile investment towards your family's good health. And you can invent easy, inexpensive ways to add fiber, protein, and vitamins. For example, our young children didn't suspect the grated cabbage mixed with the minced onion and garlic in the pasta sauce, or the spoonful of dry powdered milk that fluffed the scrambled eggs or plumped the meat patty with extra protein. Herbs and spices can replace artificial flavorings and some of the salt and sugar used for flavor.

Kids can learn healthy eating habits and self-discipline if they see that sugary drinks and goodies might be okay for an occasional sugar splurge rather than a regular jolt to the system. They also notice if it takes a double blast of caffeine at Moondollars to rev mom up for the day's routine. Some moms laughingly relate to the gift shop sign, "Without caffeine I would have no personality at all."

Fixing healthy meals for your husband rather than tempting his taste buds with fat and sugar-loaded dishes and baked goods is another way of "doing him good." He still enjoys some of his fattening favorites, but also tasty, satisfying dishes without some of the calories and cholesterol.

Working In and Out

Fresh air and exercise also came naturally through tasks such as readying raw textiles, walking to market, grinding grain, kneading dough, carrying water, and kneading clothes to clean them. Friends surprised me with a water pitcher they purchased in Bethlehem, near Rachel's tomb. The thick clay pitcher is about 11½ inches tall, 6½ inches around the middle, has a handle on one side, and filling it up to its one inch spout, holds two quarts of liquid. Carrying even this size pitcher would provide arm and aerobic exercise for the young women.

Today many girls work towards healthy womanhood by learning to like fruits and vegetables, getting fresh air and extra exercise, and refusing to deplete health and strength in worthless mind and body draining activities. Young married women keep their hearts pumping dashing from chores to children to kitchen, adding exercise through activities such as walking, biking, and flower and vegetable gardening.

Some women hike in the woods, while for others a walk around the evergreen aisle at the local big box is tiring. Some lift weights while others struggle to lift a baby or a sack of groceries. Many with limited strength deep breathe, stretch, do isometrics and chair exercises. The stronger sometimes jog, or go to a gym. Either can get instruction from books, TV, magazines or online. There are many resources to help fit exercise to ability.

If able you can work off spurts of worry or frustration with extra activity. Some run, walk, or scrub floors. I prune—very relaxing for me, though maybe not so much for the shrinking rhodys or rose bushes, or for my husband when he sees my whack job.

High Priced Spread

"Wait for me," I called, running, flapping my arms after the Canadian geese as they flew free into the reddening Salem sunrise. My husband laughed, knowing this was my silly way of saying I was "stressed out" and wanted to fly away after three weeks of emotionally and physically draining work, not of our doing, had landed in our laps.

Stress affects health. Environment, life, lifestyle, grief, fear, surgery, illness, accident, and attitude can all contribute to stress. Each person's portion of physical and emotional stress and the makeup to cope with it is different. Wouldn't life be simpler if you could just say, "Today I'm cutting out sugar, salt, and stress"?

Some stress attacks you. Other is self-inflicted. Learning to know the difference and react in the wisest way helps lessen the ill effects of strength-sapping stress. Going through every day as if braced for a strong wind when there's only a breeze, drains you. Then when adversity blows in, you might be too winded to stand up to it.

Young wives and mothers often exercise and eat right, but when they need to rest, they give their children naps and keep whipping themselves along. Usually they have good reasons: someone to do for; a project to start; work to finish; or, though already tense with fatigue, a new hobby they hope to be relaxing.

Positive plans and interesting activities energize you, but when you enjoy them and look forward to the finish, it's easy to psych yourself up after you've physically fizzled out. It took years for me to figure out that my body's persistent complaints that five babies, two miscarriages, and five major surgeries in ten years subtracted from physical strength, not added to it. Since math was never a strong point I was a slow learner.

Continually spreading yourself too thin when your body craves rest can bring a high price of poor health. Worked up or overworked mind and muscles wind up. When you unwind, tight muscles loosen, the mind calms, and you feel a peaceful sense of well-being. Psalm 127.2 gives eloquent admonition on overdoing: "It is vain for you to rise up early: To take rest late, to eat the bread of toil for so he giveth unto his beloved sleep."

When mind and muscles are stressed tight you can go from peace to panicky in seconds. Going from panicky to peace might take longer. Psalm 37 calms when people, plans, or impatience keep you stirred up. "Do not fret because of evil doers." "Trust in Jehovah and do good." "Rest in Jehovah, and wait patiently for him" it soothes. "Better is a little that the righteous hath than the abundance of many wicked...." "For there is a happy end to the man of peace."

Good Medicine

"A cheerful heart is a good medicine" (Prov 17.22). This Biblical truth is backed by medical science. Heart chiming cheer is "good" for the ill or stressed mind and body. When your heart is cheerful you sing, count your blessings, and enjoy your loved ones and your work. You feel better. You smile more. You cheer the hearts of those you smile at as they smile back.

You can be lighthearted without being lightheaded. Ecclesiastes 3.4 says "there is a time to laugh..." A cheerful heart helps you enjoy a joke, or look for some humor in hard times. It cheers your years and those who live them with you. A cousin wrote that her 100 year old mother, my Aunt Berdena, "still has her sense of humor." Hanging onto your sense of humor helps you hang in there when you want to drop out. Laughter is physically relaxing. It interrupts anxiety.

"In Nothing Be Anxious"

Anxiety can overwhelm you or hover like a low-grade fever. Philippians 4.4–7 shows prayer's powerful impact on anxiety. First Paul through inspiration, tells the Christians at Philippi to "Rejoice... always." He wasn't writing from a recliner in a bright, warm, roomy house telling persecuted Christians to cheer up. Rather, from a dim, damp, cramped Roman prison cell Paul writes, "Again, I will say rejoice." In between "Rejoice" and "Rejoice," he begins to reveal the how to.

He starts with three words that elevate joy above the earthly: "in the Lord" (Gal 3.27), the true source of genuine joy. When "in the Lord" you can rejoice regardless of the potential for earthly anxiety. But "rejoice" "always"? How? Your relationship "in the Lord" is always awesome reason to rejoice no matter what rages around you.

Then, "forbearance..." (v 5). True joy helps you let others know the Lord is always near, now and forever, to bear you up, to strengthen your gentleness, even toward those who attempt to terrorize your peace.

Next, verse 6: "In nothing be anxious." How is that possible, Paul? In "nothing"? He answers, "but in everything by prayer...." Our heartfelt appeal to the one who responds beyond what we can "ask or think" (Eph 3.20). The more we let prayer take us triumphantly through trials, the quicker we turn to prayer the next time. And it's easier to keep your chin up when your head is bowed.

Still, we often marinate our minds in misery, then think to pray. For many years Philippians 4.4–9 has instructed, cheered, comforted and strengthened me through sorrows, major surgeries, Sjogren's, and a stroke. I've also silently recited these verses to lesser stress like the screech of the dentist's drill and the clankety-clank of the MRI machine aimed at my brain. Yet I sometimes have to rebuke myself, as on the night I wrote these words, first in my mind as I lived them.

> Here I lie the livelong night
> Looking something of a fright.
> Eyes all red.
> Rumpled bed.
> Fearsome thoughts within my head.
> Why don't I pray instead?

"...and supplication." This is thoughtful, fervent, thanking, praising prayer, not just whining to the Lord.

Next, Paul jolts us with the unexpected "with thanksgiving." Be thankful at a time like this? Yes. Thanksgiving joys the heart. The mental transformation to thinking thankfully helps wipe out worry before it wipes you out. It changes your focus from "Poor me," to God's goodness.

Thanking the all-powerful God for the spiritual, earthly, and yes, even the yet unseen blessings in present sorrow and trials, "in everything," transforms your mind. Then, when Satan tries to mind-wrestle your peace from you, "the peace of God" as a spiritual sentinel, "will guard your hearts and your thoughts in Christ Jesus...." (v 7)—a peace beyond comprehension.

Beginning in verse 8 this passage even gives you "things" to "think on" to guarantee such peace: things that are true, honorable, just, pure, lovely, of good report, virtuous, and praiseworthy.

Imagine that! If in Christ, with prayerful, thankful hearts, you "think on" things of excellence instead of worrisome imaginings, and "do" the right thing, whether experiencing heartache or happiness, poor times or plenty, pain or reprieve, loneliness or fellowship, longing or fulfillment, illness or health, the "God of peace" will be with you.

Taking Inventory

Next we go to verse 18 and ask "is the worthy woman taking her New Year's inventory"? If so, she has reason to celebrate for she "perceiveth that her merchandise is profitable." She checks the tall clay jars that line the room's thick walls and delights in the golden olive oil, and the layers of wheat grains. She savors the scent of the cinnamon and the pungent coriander seeds. Earthenware bowls of pink-red pistachio nuts add brightness as she sifts small barley grains through her fingers, assessing the supply until the next harvest time. Smooth, amber honey contrasts with baskets of wrinkly raisins and figs and pots of coarse salt. Yes, there are enough pitchers for the maidens to carry water from the cistern, and goat-skin butter churns hang ready for their willing hands.

The worthy woman continues through her house. This isn't just our January jolt of enthusiasm prompting optimistic resolutions and short-lived goals. She uses both hindsight and forethought to assess the results of her many faceted activities and the possibilities for the foreseeable future. "Her gain is good" (NASB). The pink buds forming on the almond trees forecast an early spring, and the worthy woman rejoices. "In the day of prosperity be joyful…" (Ecc 7.14).

"And God Saw That It Was Good"

Genesis chapter 1 shows our creator, the creator of the amazing world we live and love and work in, experiencing a sense of satisfaction. Upon completion of each phase of creation, "God saw that it was good" (Gen 1.4, 10, 12, 18, 21, 25). Then verse 31 proclaims, "And God saw everything that he had made, and behold it was very good."

We can't compare the humble work of human hands with God's work or even comprehend His magnificent creation (Ecc 3.11), but our capacity to "enjoy good" in our work is "from the hand of God" (Ecc 2.24; 3.13).

Just as the worthy woman surveys the results of her labor and sees that her gain "is good," take time to take inventory of each area of your life to assess your gain.

Rejoice in it. It is the "gift of God."

Spiritual Storehouse

The worthy woman would also take inventory of her spiritual storehouse. A personal appraisal reveals if our inner "merchandise" is "profitable," and if our "gain is good."

We gain spiritually when we keep our "fruit of the spirit" pantry well stocked. Galatians 5.22–23 displays row upon row of the bounty available: "Love, joy, peace, long suffering, kindness, goodness, faithfulness, meekness, self-control." We can't jar joy or rush to the supermarket for five pounds of peace, a can of self-control, or a carton of faith. But high quality goods are heart ready through studying God's always in season word that fills us with the "fruits of righteousness" (Phil 1.11).

Taking stock also shows what is past date. Galatians 5.19–21 lists things that should have expired but might still be taking up spiritual space, and Colossians 2.8 helps check for spoilage. Are we being selective in the media marketplace or is rotten "merchandise" crowding "good gain" off our spiritual shelves?

Objective inventory keeps material profit off the top of the shopping list when it's just a loss leader. Matthew 16.26 helps take spiritual stock of each area of our lives: "For what profit is it to a man if he gains the whole world, and loses his own soul?" Let's take stock and enjoy "good gain."

Lamplighters

Assessing her profitable merchandise motivates the worthy woman to put her good gain to good use. "Her lamp goeth not out by night." Since their small lamps needed constant refilling, a lamplight "by night" signaled industry and preparedness.

The lamp that shone from the worthy woman's lampstand was probably a simple, palm-sized pottery bowl to hold the olive oil, crimped on one side to secure the wick. One end of the wick soaked in the oil while the crimp held the other end for lighting. Potters shaped later lamps like narrow, enclosed shoes. Ancients poured oil in a nickel-sized hole at the top of the heel end and placed the wick in the tiny opening at the toe end. Friends brought us a lamp of each type from their visit to Israel.

During our 1996 Bible lands tour we gulped falafel, then while our group lunched more leisurely, Ferrell Jenkins, tour director and friend, quickly and expertly guided Al and me through Old City Jerusalem's narrow streets to a King David Street shop. There we purchased a 2000 year old lamp of the Herodian period, the time of Christ. This small, round, earth colored lamp has a quarter-sized, oil-ready opening at the top and a thick wick rest on one side, curving up from the flat base.

It's fun to hold these rough little lamps and imagine a woman of Old or New Testament times pouring the oil, lighting the wicks, and working by the dim light as "She layeth her hands to the distaff, and her hands hold the spindle" (v 19).

Spinning

Seeing a spinning wheel sets my mind spinning. It spins 3,000 years backward and unwinds before a woman gracefully performing the ancient art of spinning. The modern spinning wheel's appeal isn't only in the warm wood, artful and efficient design, or the spun thread, but the vistas it spins up, such as the worthy woman spinning thread for daily use and a lifetime of character and purpose for our learning.

Envision a woman of old holding under her left arm the distaff—the long, smooth stick that holds the fibers—her fingers twisting the short fibers together for the spinning motion of the spindle, the weighted stick tapered toward each end, and held by her right hand.

From chapter 4 revisit the "wise-hearted" women of Exodus 35 as they willingly laid their hands to the distaff and their hands held the spindle. Read again what they spun with their simple system. "...the blue, the purple, the scarlet, and the fine linen."

The drop spindle, a smooth stick, notched near the top to hold the thread, and a stone or clay whorl, or weight at the bottom to set it spinning in a top-like motion to twist the thread, was also used by young girls as they walked about the village or sat tending the family sheep. Some cultures use this simple, yet ingenious method today because of its portability.

For years I have enjoyed watching artisans at the Oregon State Fair demonstrate spinning methods, from the drop spindle to the later, larger spinning wheels, with their admirably coordinated actions: the left hand working the distaff, the right hand controlling the thread, while the feet work the treadle.

During a trip to Florida I delighted in watching our fifteen-year-old, golden-haired granddaughter skillfully spinning grey woolen thread seated beside her frugally purchased spinning wheel made from black PVC pipe.

The Distaff Side

Since spinning was mostly done by women, "distaff" came to be used for the female sex, or feminine side of a family. Centuries later it is still used in this way.

Some feel there is also more to the word "distaff" in verse 17 than a simple tool for spinning. For example, from the Pulpit Commentary, "the Septuagint translates, she stretches out her arms to useful works." Either concept demonstrates the Four Ws as the Worthy Woman Willingly reaches for and clasps her important Work.

Jesus used spinning to challenge the disciples perspective: "And why are ye anxious concerning raiment? Consider the lilies of the field, how they grow. They toil not, neither do they spin; yet

I say unto you, that even Solomon in all his glory was not arrayed like one of these" (Matt 6.28–29, Luke 12.27).

The worthy woman's example also challenges as she uses her strength and skills for useful works, an example to her handmaidens (Psa 123.2) and women today.

Questions

1. What do the verbs in Proverbs 31.17 say about the worthy woman's approach to her physical strength?

2. From Philippians 4.6, what spiritual blessing helps us obey the command "in nothing be anxious"?

3. How can we increase our ability to perceive what is "profitable"?

4. What qualities do the wise virgins of Matthew 25.1–4 and the worthy woman share?

Strength Training

1. Memorize Psalm 23. Note the way "my," "me," and "I" make it personal.

2. Let it seep into your soul, ever ready as The Lord leads you through this life and on into eternity.

Worthy Woman
The Poor Widow

It was the last week of Christ's life in the days of Passover, in the city of Jerusalem. Jesus was teaching in the temple as only He could teach—preaching the gospel, speaking parables, answering crafty questions from Pharisees, Herodians, Saducees, warning of the scribes, including their treatment of widows.

He looked up and saw the people casting their gifts into the treasury. "Many that were rich cast in much." Then a "certain" woman caught His attention. "There came a poor widow and she cast in two mites" (about ½ of a cent).

Jesus gathered his disciples and taught them a profound lesson from her simple act. "This poor widow cast in more than all they that are casting into the treasury, for the rich gave out of their abundance, but she of her want did cast in all that she had, even all her living." They gave easily of their excess, but she gave with all her "mite."

We can only speculate on the journey that led her to poverty, but her heart had arrived with the "all" approach to life. Perhaps she had a priorities perspective even as a young wife. Her husband may have left her a good example in giving the Jew's requirement of ten percent, or even more. Maybe as a married woman she had heard and taken to heart the story of Elisha filling pots of oil for the poor widow so the creditor would not take her sons. Had this poor widow struggled raising children alone? Whatever her experience as a widow, whether loss of a loving husband, loneliness, or financial hardship, she allowed it to enrich her spirit.

When I once commended an older widow for giving so much of herself to her congregation she said, "After my husband died I made up my mind I wasn't going to be a dead widow." The poor widow of Mark 12 didn't withdraw from life saying, "What could I, a poor widow do?" She "came" and "cast in" more than all the others. An "all" attitude is evident in many areas. Some may be rich in talent, time, strength, or money and "cast in much" out of their surplus, while others seem to give or do little, but the Lord sees and knows it is their "all."

By most standards the poor widow's mite would not merit remembrance. But through inspiration two of the gospels, Mark 12.41–44 and Luke 21.1–4, immortalize this moment, a lasting lesson and tribute to the all-out willing giving of a worthy widow.

Facets
Footsteps
My husband and I felt privileged to walk in the land of Israel knowing Jesus our Lord had walked there, knowing that 2,000 years ago, as His sandals imprinted the dusty soil, His profound yet simple teaching and perfect example made deep impressions on the hearts and minds of many and redirected their steps.

Knowing He taught truths from fishing boats much like the rare "Galilee Boat" we had viewed. Knowing He crossed this same Sea of Galilee we were crossing in them. Knowing He walked on these waters. We were shivering. Not just from the damp morning mist, the cool breeze rippling the waters around our boat, or the blending of our hearts and voices as our group of Christians sang, "Peace. Be Still."

How exhilarating and humbling it was to walk in Israel knowing Jesus walked, taught, and performed "mighty works" there. Knowing He was raised from the dead to once again walk and awaken the hearts of men with His teaching.

Walking where Jesus walked awakens our souls and inspires us to walk as He walked. I have walked where Jesus lived, but do I live for Jesus? I have walked in the excavated streets of Bethsaida, but am I walking in "newness of life"? Do I walk in love? Do I wail at the wall of unforgiveness? Am I walking in the truth? Do I "walk by faith"? Do I strive to "walk worthily of the Lord? " Jesus left a forever footprint that we may walk in "His steps" (Rom 6.4; Eph 4.1, 32; John 15.12; 2 Cor 5.7; Col 1.10; 1 Pet 2.21).

SEVEN

She stretcheth out her hand to the poor;
Yea, she reacheth forth her
hands to the needy.

We inched along on an icy street in heavy traffic. Curbside a man held up a WILL WORK FOR FOOD sign with weather-reddened hands. The driver ahead of us rolled down his window, took off his gloves, and stretched them out the window to the cold man on the curb. The sign holder put down his sign, put on the gloves, then with a "Thank you" wave of his now gloved hands acknowledged this heart to hand act of kindness. The glove giver had literally stretched out his hand to another human being with what he had at hand.

The worthy woman of Proverbs 31.20 "stretcheth out her hand to the poor."

Her life demonstrated Ephesians 4.28, "...but rather let him labor, working with his hands, the thing that is good, that he may have whereof to give to him that hath need." People of character and compassion can't go smugly on their way knowing someone else is miserable. Instead, they honor the urge to help if it is within their power. No hands off, "I've made my way and so can they" attitude. Thoughts centered on ourselves in self-pity or selfishness shrivel our emotions. Care and concern for others plump up our hearts and stretch our hands right out of our comfort zone.

The generous woman of our study didn't use her "gain" for show or selfishness as did Jerusalem who justified and selfishly out-sinned her sister cities. "Behold, this was the iniquity of thy sister Sodom: Pride, fullness of bread, and prosperous ease was in her and her daughters; neither did she strengthen the hand of the poor and needy" (Ezek 16.49–51).

Shared Gleanings

Compassion is written right into the Old Testament harvest laws. The gleanings of the sheaf, the olive trees, and the grapes were for the "stranger, the fatherless, and the widow" (Deut 24.19–21). Leviticus 19.9–10 instructs the Israelites to leave the gleanings and fallen fruit for the poor and the sojourner. In her time, those in need could count on the worthy woman's family fields and vineyards for gleanings (Prov 31.20).

The well-known gleaner, Ruth, said to the servant in charge of the reapers: "Let me glean, I pray you, and gather after the reapers among the sheaves" (Ruth 2.7). She showed humility by asking for and accepting help; then, though widowed and poor herself, she showed character and compassion by sharing her gleanings with Naomi.

Heart and Hands On

"Yea, she reacheth forth her hands to the needy." Some scholars say that the plural "hands" suggests personal involvement, and "hand" conveys the idea of giving alms, or money. First Timothy 6.17–19 instructs the rich in this good work.

Those the worthy woman helped weren't just on her To-Do list, they were on her heart. "If there is among you a poor man of your brethren…you shall not harden your heart nor shut your hand from your poor brother, but you shall open your hand wide to him" (Deut 15.7–8). Her heart and hands were wide open.

James 2.15 asks, "If a brother or sister is naked and destitute of daily food, and one of you says to them 'Depart in peace, be warmed and filled'; but you do not give them the things which are needed for the body, what does it profit?" Empty words don't fill needs.

Dorcas combined "almsdeeds," which included both financial help and the work of her own hands, into one life "full of good works" (Acts 9.36). She used her workmanship to demonstrate His workmanship. "For we are His workmanship, created in Christ Jesus for good works" (Eph 2.10).

"Good Eye"

"Put on a heart of compassion, kindness…" (Col 3.12). A kind, compassionate heart causes you to stretch and reach to clasp hearts and hands with hurting people. Proverbs 22.9 helps lengthen our stretch and reach. "He who has a bountiful eye shall be blessed; for he gives of his bread to the poor." The footnote for "bountiful" in the ASV and "generous" in the NKJV is "good." A "good" eye, an eye for doing good, lengthens your reach.

When our four sons played Little League, if a player hit a good pitch or passed on a bad one, coaches and parents yelled, "Good eye!" Look around with a "good eye" for doing good—someone with a legitimate need.

Does your "good eye" see someone with a financial need but too embarrassed to ask? An elderly lady often asked, "Do you know if 'so and so' needs anything?" If they did, Juanita always had a little money ready for gas or groceries. Years of stretching out her hand trained her "good eye" for perceiving needs.

Can your "good eye" spot a lonely sister? She feels a flu-like ache, only it's inside and won't go away in a week or two. Maybe you can spot a new Christian who needs a friend, or help with Bible studies? A lonely classmate? A single or overwhelmed mom? Someone new in town?

Have a good eye for one still grieving, putting on a happy face to cheer others, though she still feels overwhelmed. Does she need someone to listen, or remember her loved one with her? Not to "sing songs to a heavy heart." Though the singer means well, a chirpy tune to the grieving "is as one who takes away your coat in cold weather, or vinegar fizzing on soda" (Prov 25.20).

Or do you see someone whose husband isn't a Christian? Once, when inviting a group over, I asked an older woman whose husband wasn't a Christian to bring him too. This reserved lady wept. "He wouldn't come with me, and he doesn't like me to go without him." Though she rarely missed Bible classes or assemblies, she longed for other together times with fellow Christians.

Look for those struggling with illness: short-term, chronic, or terminal. Do they need a vacuum pushed? Groceries? An outing for the children? A ride to the doctor? Are they in pain, feeling useless, misunderstood, or left out? Can you empathize into their bedroom slippers?

Personal suffering can open your eyes to others. For example, as with other adversity, illness and limitation at a young age gives you early insight into old age. It stretches your heart and hands to help, comfort, and share the source of your comfort. "Blessed be the God and Father of our Lord Jesus Christ, the Father of mercies and God of all comfort; who comforts us in all our tribulation, that we may be able to comfort those that are in any trouble, with the comfort with which we ourselves are comforted by God (2 Cor 1.3–4 NKJV).

Short Reach

The seagull took a stare-down stance on a jagged rock above the crashing waves, giving us the "eagle eye" like an eagle wannabe. People can, with assumed authority, pridefully prejudge others on a superficial basis from race to rations. "They don't look poor to me." Most people don't try to "look poor" and might even have a talent for making the most of what they do have so they won't.

Some size up the sick. "They don't look sick." Many illnesses don't come with outward signs, and most sick people try not to "look sick." Others shorten their reach because, "They look to me like they're holding up okay." Some people "look okay" even during a crisis. Concerned hearts will talk to the people of concern so they won't be overlooked.

We've probably all shortened our reach with, "I wanted to help, but I didn't know what to do." Our own experience helps us imagine another's. Are you a mom? You can picture a sick mother's young child hungry for breakfast or needing a ride from school.

Got a grandma? Would another older woman have similar needs? Ever spent long days at a hospital with a loved one? You know how some sandwiches or, "We care cookies" might help. Can't fix a whole meal for a sick family? Some muffins or a hot dish, a hearty soup, or a pasta salad might furnish chew and cheer.

Too Young

"I'm too young," can shorten your reach. Many pre-teen and teenage girls reach out to bake cookies, write cards, help with child or pet care, or clean for others. Boys also stretch to replace light bulbs, mow lawns, help people move, and visit the elderly. Many young people reach out to those who don't know Christ. I'm probably a Christian because an older teenager up our country road asked me to Sunday worship with her. Helen's parents were among those who had a part in my parents, then in their forties, becoming Christians.

Young mothers can feel "too young" to reach out as they care for husband and children, keep up with busy schedules, and undergo their own family calamities. When our house was buzzing with our five young children, my 41-year-old brother died when his pickup went over a cliff. Then my father suffered with lung cancer for over five years, and died at age sixty-nine. During these times it might be easy to think women whose children are older or grown must always have ever-ready houses, full cupboards, and empty schedules—until you get there, and see that middle-aged and older women's lives can be complicated and calamity filled as well.

During one stretch of our lives Al's father had Alzheimer's for three years, then died, my mother died of pneumonia after her second leg amputation, and Al's mother was bedfast and unable to speak for two years before her death because of strokes. His 51-year-old sister died of a brain tumor before his mother's death.

Meanwhile, we had ordinary family activities and responsibilities, confronted other illnesses, got younger children off to college, and married, took part in the joys and struggles of others, and Al continued to preach and teach full time. We often felt stretched too thin in some areas, and our reach shortened in others. Many relate, thankful for God-given strength and the prayers and support of fellow Christians, as difficult times sometimes phase in and forget to phase out.

Both old and young usually have full lives. Many young married women stretch out with strong, sinewy souls to the needs of their families, fellow Christians, neighbors, and others. Young deacon's wives are often involved in needs not all are aware of, and many young preachers' wives reach out to responsibilities beyond the scope and awareness of others their age. Some even reach beyond the seas.

Too Old?

Older women can shorten their reach by saying, "I'm too old," or "I've done my share," or, forgetting how full a younger woman's life can be, "It's the young women's turn." But most older women use their "Can do" attitudes and physical abilities to keep stretching and reaching out. Some less mobile, or weaker physically, reach out through their phones, computers, and mailboxes—often in creative ways.

One day when our nest was still full, the mailman brought an envelope addressed with a weak hand and no return address. It contained a ten dollar bill and a grocery store coupon advertising, "One dozen roses-$9.99." When I was well enough I traded the ten dollar bill and the Safeway coupon for 12 bright pink roses, then called a frail, elderly lady and asked, "Did I get something in the mail from you?" I thanked her and described the cheerful bouquet. Fern was glad I "didn't get something practical with the money," and I was impressed and uplifted by her creative compassion. (Worthy Women Of Today, Ch. 13, salutes the willing hearts and hands of women of all ages)

Sold Short

Do you sell your long reach short? Women of all ages do. Many hurry to help relieve heart and hunger pains and serve in other ways, yet feel useless or wish for a talent. They overlook their many gifts, such as having an eye for encouragement. Some kindly encourage young and old, the widowed, the sick, those out of work, the depressed, the elders, evangelists, deacons, and others.

Some are good listeners. Women confide their sorrows and dilemmas to them knowing they will listen, pray, and check back on their heartaches. Loving hearts show loving kindness to those in nursing homes, taking care of small needs that help them retain their dignity.

Many, such as Epaphras, "labor fervently...in prayers" (Col 4.12), perhaps more so than more able-bodied sisters who help many but might be more distracted from prayer. Others are on automatic invite, inviting people to assemblies, classes, and gospel meetings. Some hearten others with thoughtful cards and notes (Prov 25.25), like Elaine whose handmade cards, like her life, are lovely, artistic, and uplifting.

Congregations worldwide appreciate each woman, regardless of age, who is as Paul described Phoebe, "A helper of many" (Rom 16.2).

Balance

The many opportunities to stretch and reach out lead to the question of balance. Doing enough? Too much? Do-gooders or doing "good works?" A woman complained to a columnist that a friend "knocked herself out helping others," cooking elaborate dinners for other families, while her own children looked after themselves, eating sandwiches in a messy house.

When are we neglecting our families and when James 4.17? "Therefore, to him who knows to do good and does not do it, to him it is sin" (NKJV). And, though worldwide poverty will never be eliminated (Deut 15.11, Mark 14.7), where should we aim our efforts?

Which needs should we stretch toward? And what about the human tendency to feel tired and put upon when our own arms need lifting up? How do circumstances fit with Galatians 6.9–10? "And let us not be weary in well-doing; for in due season we shall reap, if we faint not."

Maybe we overextend because we can't say "No," or pride

pushes us along. Many women live Christ-centered lives, carefully care for their families, help others also, but but still carry a black bag of guilt on their backs because of others they didn't help.

I don't presume to have adequate answers to these age old uncertainties but hope these thoughts will help. Common sense considers present abilities and responsibilities, and the desire and capacity to do more. Are there other factors?

The worthy woman provides an ideal example for personal benevolence. She was wise, kind, healthy, wealthy, eager and organized. Her depth of wisdom, multifaceted activities, and a "known in the gates" husband make it unlikely she was a young woman.

The younger woman learning to love her husband, love and care for her children, grow in inner qualities, and outer awareness of others, has a shorter outward reach. Some, kindly perceptive to the needs of others, think their own family responsibilities hinder their "good works." Titus 2.3–5 reminds that husband and children are central to "that which is good" to the young wife and mother. Younger wives and mothers should, can, and do stretch and reach out to each other and others, but it takes balance, and for some years the scale will tip towards the family.

It seems that according to Scripture and normal circumstances, the ideal approach to benevolence is with the older woman leading and the younger learning. The older woman's experience brings insight. When I was a young married woman of 19, an older woman took me to help a friend dying of cancer. Since I hadn't seen serious illness in others, and didn't know how to help with her pain or personal care, I did household chores, watching and learning as La Verne knew just what to say and do for our friend.

Older women teach through attitude as well as action. After a hospital stay to recover from a miscarriage, an older woman insisted I recuperate in her home for a few days. When we tried to thank her Beth said, "Just help someone else when you're able."

When a congregation has loving, eager, active, spiritually mature older women who realize the importance of their service to God, their families, fellow Christians, and fellowman, it is blessed.

As these women are alert to opportunities to serve, including and encouraging the younger women to lengthen their reach, they are training the next generation in kindness to others (Tit 2.4).

Usually, each age group has willing workers who also could be commended by Mark 14.4: "She hath done what she could." Review the special networking system described in chapter three that furthers the powerful older-younger woman combination of love and good works.

Given to Hospitality

The worthy woman reached out with both arms to give hospitality a hug. Though many examples already mentioned are included in hospitality, it merits special attention. Scripture says to stretch and reach toward this good work.

For "given to hospitality" (Rom 12.13), the footnote says "pursuing," or seeking eagerly after. Genesis 18.1–7 shows Abraham eagerly showing hospitality to three messengers of God as he has Sarah make cakes and he runs to fetch a calf for their meal. "Forget not to show love unto strangers: for thereby some have entertained angels unawares" (Heb 13.2).

Whenever Elisha was in the area the "great woman of Shunem" expressed hospitality by inviting him to eat. Then, perceiving that Elisha was a man of God, she talked to her husband about preparing a room, furnishing it with a bed, table, seat, and a candlestick so Elisha and his servant would have a place to stay whenever they were traveling nearby (2 Kgs 4.8–10).

"The stranger that sojourneth with you shall be unto you as the home-born" (Lev 19.34). The Israelites empathized with travelers for they had been "sojourners" in the land of Egypt. Their hospitality helped the stranger and sojourner who traveled by foot over hot, dusty roads, and knew inns could be crowded, unsafe, and of ill repute.

Today's traveler often has a car, motel room, or motor home. But there are "sojourners," such as someone new to the area, someone visiting the assembly, or new Christians to reach out to and make feel at home. Within a congregation, members who enjoy a welcoming circle of family and friends can look around after the service or class, and reach out so that a stranger doesn't leave looking like a half-starved coyote while the "home-born" feast on their fellowship.

Special Interest Group

Galatians 6.10 shows Christians who to reach and stretch toward: "…all men and especially toward them that are of the household of faith."

First Peter 4.9 shows how: "Without grumbling" (NKJV). First Peter 1.22 combines who, how, and why: "Seeing ye have purified your souls in your obedience to the truth unto unfeigned love of the brethren, love one another from the heart fervently." Knowing and obeying the truth leads to sincere, heartfelt, loving acts of kindness to each other.

The importance of hospitality within a congregation is emphasized by its place in the qualifications for elders. They are to be "given to" hospitality (Tit 1.8; 1 Tim 3.2). Elders' wives can encourage and assist their husband in this responsibility within the congregation and often do in ways both known and unknown to others.

Reach or Retreat

The subject of at-home hospitality brings mixed reactions. "We need new furniture first," says a young wife. "With the price of food who can afford it?" asks a middle-income mother of one. "I've never learned to entertain graciously," says an older woman with a lovely home and grown children. "It's easy for you," says another naively, "you're a preacher's wife." Many who don't embrace hospitality say, "We're too busy."

Most can relate. It does take extra doing, redoing schedules, extra groceries, and maybe scrunching up and bumping elbows at the table. But hiding in the above quotes, and shushing the "I'd Like Tos" is often a sense of uncertainty. Some say they've even "been part way ready for company" then let fear paralyze their plans.

Who hasn't felt the pre-guest jitters? As a newlywed of two months I found myself planning dinner for a visiting preacher and his family. Wishing for family to practice on, I searched my bridal shower Betty Crocker cookbook for recipes that fit our limited budget and my new bride cooking skills, then started rattling the pots and pans. Our guests arrived and all went well. My fears had been unfounded. I'd like to add that all entertaining came easily ever after—but who would believe it? We enjoyed our guests, though, and I gained confidence for the future.

This type of hospitality continued to enrich our lives such as when the man who wrote the forward for the original *A Worthy Woman* first stayed with us. Busy with a two- and three-year-old, I was nervous about keeping brother Hailey, a well-known preacher, author, and my husband's college professor, but soon saw why my husband loved and respected this vibrant man so much. His plain-spoken vitality both in and out of the pulpit, his Bible knowledge, ability to quote lengthy passages of Scripture, his kindness, and humor. My feelings of inadequacy could have cheated us out of this rewarding experience and later visits.

An interesting experience in sharing our home was when, in helping start a new congregation in a new area, the church met in our home for a year-and-a-half. This was a challenge since we met three times a week and even used our five- and three-year-old's bedroom for a classroom, but the rewards outweighed the work.

Hospitality also teaches that you don't always know what appeals to a person. When we had teenagers, a young man invited three others, who appeared to have had a rougher life than many, to the young people's class in our home. We invited them all into the family room where we thought the group would feel the most at home. Later, during refreshments, I noticed the three were missing. I found them in the then set apart living room. One said, "This is so nice and peaceful, we just had to sit in here awhile."

Your Way

Opportunities for hospitality are many, from the stranger and the poor to well-fed friends and family. The ways to bring it about are as varied as the hands and hearts that do.

List making and fix-ahead food helps you enjoy company

without being too busy in the kitchen. A sense of humor helps too, such as when someone dropped the gravy boat in the salad bowl, creating a unique house dressing. An icebreaker was when an oven light bulb exploded, ruining a batch of biscuits big enough for our five guests and the seven of us.

After an illness short-circuited my strength I wanted to catch up with more people at a time, groups for refreshments or finger foods was an enjoyable, easier way to reach out, but one table full where you get to know each other eyeball to eyeball is still a favorite. Adapt to your capabilities and circumstances so reaching out will be a joy not a job.

Many who take part in the enriching endeavor of hospitality say, "It does us more good than it does them." A single woman who enjoys getting everything ready for guests says, "It's a way that I can help." From an enthusiastic young couple who got the "hospitality habit," "It does us so much good." A gracious older couple says, "Others have helped us in the past, now we want to pass it on." Included in the openhearted, open-handed attitude of the majority is, "We want to do more." (See "Guests" at end of chapter).

Questions

1. In Proverbs 31.11, who does the worthy woman stretch and reach to?

2. Who did Jesus put on the guest list in Luke 14.12–14?

3. In Matthew 25.35–42, what did Jesus say those on His right hand, and left hand did or did not do?

4. From Ephesians 2.10, what does it mean to walk in good works?

Strength Training

1. Think about your talents and experiences that can expand your insight and input into another's needs.

2. Discuss ways to show hospitality that would be helpful to those in your congregation or community (Gal 6.10). Plan to reach out to someone in some way within the month.

3. Weight lift. Seek out others who need weight lovingly lifted from their shoulders and—pump iron.

Worthy Woman
Phoebe

"I commend unto you Phoebe..." Who is Phoebe that Paul, in his letter from Corinth to the Christians in Rome, wanted to make them aware of her? Whatever her familial, secular, or financial status, he esteemed Phoebe's "in Christ" relationship to himself and the Roman Christians and revealed it with that valued title, "our sister." Then he continues to commend her with a word that both honors and humbles Christians, "a servant."

Phoebe was a dedicated servant of the church in the port city of Cenchrea, near Greece. Paul wanted the Romans to welcome her in a manner becoming to Christians and help her with her needs while with them. "For indeed she has been a helper of many and of myself also" (NKJV).

He appreciated her work, as well as the labor of other women included in Romans 16 such as Priscilla who, along with her husband Aquila, was a fellow-worker in Christ with Paul, risked her neck for him, and opened their home to the church. His letter also greeted and praised the women "Tryphaena and Tryphosa, "who labor in the Lord," "the beloved Persis," and the mother of Rufus who had been like a mother to Paul. He also commended the men mentioned in chapter 16.1–15.

As the women welcomed and helped Phoebe, they would also be blessed with knowing her and sharing their experiences as Christian women—and they, as Paul, would give God the glory for any good done. They would not aid those who caused division and stumbling, "Who by their smooth and fair speech they beguile the hearts of the innocent" (v. 18). These women were sincere servants, laboring in the Lord.

The KJV uses "succourer," suggesting a woman of dignity, to describe Phoebe as she helped others. She and the other women Paul praises in Romans 16 were as the Proverbs 31 woman of strength and dignity, as they stretched and reached to serve others.

Facets
Guests

Go to it. Don't put it off. You might miss the opportunity to fill a hunger more important than the physical nourishment shared, and cheat your family and yourself out of an enriching experience. "Pursue hospitality" (Rom 12.13).

Use what you have. Waiting for new furniture? While you wait what you have is wearing out, and others are missing out. "So then, as we have opportunity…." (Gal 6.10).

Entertain in your own style according to your budget, tastes, strength, and skills. Best dishes or a cookout? When you're comfortable, your guests feel more comfortable. The love shown is the masterpiece of your menu (Heb 13.2).

Share your home and hospitality with the less fortunate and strangers as well as favorite friends. Loneliness isn't unique to age, race, sex, or social status (Matt 25.40).

Tone down cleaning and preparation. If you overdo it, you might never want to do it again. Mary and Martha both had hospitable hearts, but Martha overdid the extras (Luke 10.38–42).

Smile with the satisfaction of service. And start planning the next time. Home hospitality might be the specialty you've been looking for. "…there is nothing better for them than to rejoice and to do good so long as they live" (Ecc 3.12).

EIGHT

She is not afraid of the snow for her household,
For all her household are clothed with scarlet.
She maketh for herself carpets of tapestry;
Her clothing is fine linen and purple.

Mesmerized, we sit watching the fluffy whiteness of the snow lighting up the landscape and graciously covering its imperfections, thinking only of its loveliness. But for some the spellbound mood will change to snowbound reality. The excitement of the first snowman subsides and the wonder wears off, as a cold realization settles in like slush.

Not everyone is cuddled up to a cozy fire drinking hot chocolate. Hazardous driving conditions and power outages challenge many. Bitter cold leaves people shivering in homes without heat, unable to get out for food. Death will be the rescue party for others stranded in the frozen snow.

Fear chills like the bitterest cold, but the worthy woman warms with confidence. "She is not afraid of the snow for her household." As with other uncertainties, warnings of a hard winter cause uneasiness, but preparing ahead calms. Though a "time of snow" (2 Sam 23.20) wasn't common in ancient times, some had seen "snow from heaven" (Isa 55.10–11), even black ice (Job 6.16).

Prepared
The worthy woman prepared even for the unusual. An unex-

pected eight inches of snow, such as blanketed Old City Jerusalem and much of the Middle East January 30, 2008, would have found her family among those "bundled up in warm clothing," as the news described dozens of residents. They would have enjoyed the snow as a scarved, red-hatted young woman in the area who said "her heart was laughing."

Today children's hearts feel more like laughing when planning and effort is put into their clothing for school and other activities so they won't feel needlessly uncomfortable or self-conscious. Thought toward his attire can also help a husband feel more confident and less stressed.

The worthy woman feels satisfaction "for all her household are clothed with scarlet." This wasn't an unexpected snowfall of serenity. She had planned and worked ahead; gathering, spinning, and weaving. The porous wool readily absorbed the scarlet dye from the crushed eggs of the Kirmiz insect found on the oak tree. (Some called it crimson from the word kirmiz.) She would set some aside for furnishings and clothing.

Personal Projects

"She maketh for herself carpets of tapestry" (v 22). Just when we might wonder if the worthy woman ever thought of herself, verse 22 shows her taking time for personal projects and appearance. First, she makes "for herself" artistic additions for her home. "Carpets of tapestry" included pillows or cushions for seating, reclining, padding benches or couches, and for bed coverings.

She works by hand, weaving in the dyed threads. Soon the current project becomes a creative blend of texture, design, and color. Perhaps she will choose this one for her bed covering. She delights in using her "woman's touch" to make her home more comfortable and appealing.

Today's woman also becomes the artist in residence as she uses her resources, ingenuity, and feminine expertise to create an inviting atmosphere for herself and her family. Her home offers opportunity to expand her interests and talents and discover new ones to liven her home and lift spirits.

Imaginative minds constantly invent new crafts or revive and re-invent old ones. There's always a worldwide, wide-eyed fascination for home-related crafts. While at the Old Jerusalem marketplace I saw women with white head coverings framing their interested eyes as they watched sewing machine demonstrations.

Making the Most of It

You can use your home to develop a talent for today—not someday. Waiting for a new house to energize you? Brainstorm what you have while you're waiting, whether your first tiny apartment, a rental home, or your own house. Even small changes can improve looks and outlooks. Engage your imagination as you combine work and fun.

Think color. Add your personality. Subtract clutter. Group artwork, or family photos. Flip-flop furniture, whether new, old, hand-me-down, or secondhand. We still have some of our first secondhand store pieces in our living room: a small desk, then $3.00, two Queen Anne end tables, 50 cents each, caned back rocker, $2.50 (its mate given to us by fellow Christians when a congregation met in our house). Our older elbows haven't redone the finish put on by younger elbow grease, but they still sit, glued together by sentiment, in our more modern house.

Sometimes decorative touches bring heart-touching moments. One morning as I was drinking tea, our eight-year-old grandson asked, "Grandma, what does your cup say?" Together we read, "This is the day the Lord has made, we will rejoice and be glad in it" (Psa 24.18), then talked about the verse. A few minutes later: "Grandma, we're doing it." "Doing what?" I looked to where he and his younger brother were playing with Legos. "What your cup says. We're playing happy."

"The make the most of it" approach also works outside, whether a small patio or large yard. Clearance plants can often be revived with a little nurture. For years I've enjoyed using fun money from Mother's Day or birthdays for yard finds such as bird baths or benches. Still do—even in the narrow strip around this house.

Time Out for You

No time for any extras? It's worth a try. Time out time is important physically and psychologically. When you just want to grab your bowl of cherries and sit and spit pits, it's past time for a change of pace hobby or a renewed interest in an old one to cut short a "woman's work is never done" mood. For one of those changes around the house—something simple like a soak in the tub, a walk, time to read, or take a nap. When I had three babies under seventeen-and-a-half months, even a 30-minute sit and stare session was refreshing.

But you have children clinging to your knees? Involve them. They respond to variety too. They can do crafts, simple sewing, "plant fwowers," take pictures, dabble in their own paints, often revealing talents of their own. They also enjoy helping mommy bake. One young mother takes her three small daughters with their hand made cards and home baked cookies to cheer others. We've enjoyed their smiling deliveries. (See also Taking Time – End of Ch.)

Her Clothing

The worthy woman took time for herself that enhanced her home and her personal appearance. "Her clothing is fine linen and purple." The process of turning flax into linen, described in chapter four, could produce "fine linen." A fast spinning motion combined with stretching made possible a fine thread, as did pre-soaking the flax in water until it was soft.

Fine linen and purple were often associated with honor, wealth, or royalty. The coats of the priestly garments were of fine linen, and purple was used in the embroidered work (Exod 39.27–29). Tapestry hangings in the Shushan palace were fastened with sashes of "fine linen and purple" (Est 1.6). Mordecai went forth with a "robe of fine linen and purple" (Est 8.15). The rich man in Luke 16.19 "was clothed in purple and fine linen."

Dye hunters searched the Mediterranean coast for the large Purpura shellfish. From it they took a gland that oozed a garlicky smelling, deep yellow liquid, which the hot sun turned to a bright reddish purple. They also crushed smaller shellfish for the dye. The large number of the smaller ones needed and conditions such as killing the fish in fall or winter helped make the purple dye expensive.

Lydia was a "seller of purple" (Acts 16.14). Her home city of Thyatira was famous for the purple dye sold through dye plants, and as a cottage industry. Archeological digs uncovered homes equipped with dye vats. Her home was possibly on the path of the merchant caravans known to stop at homes of the wealthy, or she delivered the purple to the merchants. Her wardrobe included the expensive purple as did the worthy woman's. The appearance of both the Old Testament Ideal Woman, and the New Testament Lydia would reflect a dignified balance of quality and good taste (see ch 9).

"What Shall We Wear?"

Matthew 6.31 cautions, "Do not worry saying… 'What shall we wear?'" (NKJV). Whether we have little or lots of time, energy, or money, we can become obsessed with clothing, worrying about what to wear or going to extremes. Imagine the models featured in Isaiah 3.16–24. Do we want to fashion ourselves as the "daughters of Zion" on the runway of the ridiculous? We can fret about being put in situations in old age where we might lose our dignity, yet choose fashions that give it away before we lose it. "Be not fashioned according to this world; but be ye transformed by the renewing of your mind" (Rom 12.2).

There are many viewpoints on women's apparel. For some, culture or conscience requires covering from collar bones to ankle bones. Others, both young and old, seem comfortable with cleavage, though it makes those around them uncomfortable. Some feel modestly dressed if they're covered from their knees to their Bs, but are okay with tight or see-through.

Many young women struggle into modest clothing to meet the "chaste" challenge of Titus 2.5 while living in a society that applauds the "Hot Mom" look. From any age or view, a dismissive "If someone has a problem with the way I dress, it's their problem," doesn't dismiss the "modest apparel" of 1 Timothy 2.9.

Queen Vashti showed character and courage when she refused to show herself before the men at the king's feast. What do we show when we come to worship our King, and partake of the Lord's supper? Does our appearance "profess godliness" whenever we are in public view?

First Timothy 2.10 shows outer apparel reflects inner apparel; "which is proper for women professing godliness, with good works." (See also 1 Pet 3.3–5.) Proverbs 31.22 stands out as the one verse that describes the worthy woman's outer clothing, in contrast to the 21 verses that reveal her extensive inner wardrobe.

Questions

1. From verse 21, what caused the worthy woman's confidence?

2. How does being prepared affect our family?

3. What are some simple ways to take time out even during complicated circumstances?

4. How do inner and outer attire relate?

Strength Training

1. Weigh your circumstances against your preparedness for the expected and unexpected.

2. Think of ways to strengthen your readiness.

3. Search the scriptures that relate to, and prepare you for your life situations.

Worthy Woman
Esther

Esther, who was "lovely and beautiful," was brought to the Shushan palace with many other lovelies of the land to compete for the crown of Queen. The king's servants suggested this plan to please and appease King Ahaseurus after he ousted Queen Vasthi because she refused to be ogled by the men at the king's feast.

The appointed officers brought Esther from her simple home in the Persian valley where she was raised by her older cousin

Mordecai, a Jew, to the Shushan palace where she would see lush gardens, fine linen and purple, marble pillars, gold and silver, and a pavement of alabaster, turquoise, and black and white marble.

Outwardly eyecatching, her pleasant manner impressed Hegai, the head custodian of the women. It also likely kept the other contestants from resenting her when he favored her with extra beauty preparations, "seven choice maidservants," and moved her to the "best place in the house of the women" for the year-long preparation. Mordecai, who had cared for Esther as his own daughter after her father and mother died, "paced before the court of the women's quarters" hoping to learn of her welfare. Even the extra attention didn't turn Esther into a demanding, temperamental contestant. When her turn came to be presented before the king she asked no special favors, but relied only on Hegai's advice. "And Esther obtained favor in the sight of all who saw her."

The providence of God brought her beauty into the presence of King Ahaseurus. She "obtained grace and favor in his sight more than all the other virgins, so he set the royal crown upon her head and made her queen." Soon after, the ever alert Mordecai learned that two of the king's doormen were plotting against the king. Esther told the king, giving Mordecai credit, actions that would benefit him at a crucial time later. The doormen were hanged.

But, another conspiracy was brewing that would stretch Queen Esther's young soul. Because Mordecai would not bow before the the king's highest servant, the prideful Haman, he schemed to have him killed along with all the other Jews, both adults and little ones. King Ahaseurus agreed to Haman's wicked plan, not knowing that the Jews were Esther's people too, for Mordecai had advised her not to reveal it and she obeyed him as she had in childhood.

Mordecai mourned in sackcloth and ashes and wept bitterly. All the Jews in the one-hundred and twenty-seven provinces mourned, fasted, and wept. When Esther's handmaids and servants told her about the decree "the queen was deeply distressed." However, when Mordecai wanted her to go before the king on behalf of her people, she was afraid since she could be killed if she went without invitation and then was refused his scepter. But Mordecai's next words kindled Esther's conscience and courage: "Yet who knows whether you have come to the kingdom for such a time as this?"

Then, the still fearful but now focused Esther sent word back to Mordecai to gather the Jews in Shushan to fast for her for three days, saying she and her maidens, whom she had no doubt influenced to her ways, would do the same. "And so I will go to the king, which is against the law, and if I perish, I perish."

On the third day, with young, strength-straightened shoulders beneath her royal robe, Esther risked the crown and her life to do right for Mordecai and their people. She "stood in the inner court of the king's palace, across from the king's house, while the king sat on his royal throne facing the entrance. ...When he saw Queen Esther...she found favor in his sight...and held out to her the golden scepter. ...Esther went near and touched the top of it." When the king asked Esther her requests she did not squander his generosity on selfish pursuits but seized the opportunity to pursue a plan to save her people.

Her plan was aided when the king heard again the record of his scheming doormen and remembered Mordeci for future honor for revealing their plot. Then Esther told the king of Haman's devious plan to kill the Jews, which included her and Mordecai, and Haman was hanged. Mordecai was given his position, and the Jewish people were given permission to defend themselves against assault resulting from the decree to kill them. Their lives were saved.

Unlike the self-seeking murderous Haman, Mordecai, now second to King Ahaseurus, "was great among the Jews and well received by the multitude of his brethren, seeking the good of his people and speaking peace to all his countrymen."

The lovely, orphaned Esther, though thrust into a lifestyle she had not asked for and may not have wanted, marrying a man she may have respected only for his position as husband and king, showed impressive strength of character.

She could have vainly flaunted her beauty and allowed the

prestige of the queen's crown and the prospect of personal pleasure to make her disrespect the good done for her by good people and Mordecai's fatherly care of her. She could have put fear before him and the rest of her people.

Instead, she acted worthily, according to Mordecai's advice and the best of her young wisdom, strength, and knowledge. Down through the ages Esther has inspired women of all ages to put themselves aside, put on their royal robes of courage, and do the right thing.

Today, standing before our king, we can put on a cape of courage and stand for right, asking ourselves "Who knows whether you have come to the kingdom for such a time as this?" (The Book of Esther)

Facets
Taking Time

Time for a break? Finding time can be a creative challenge. But, ten minutes here, twenty minutes there, and you've planned a project, researched it, or played at it.

Or, you've used those minutes to let your muscles loosen, your mind untangle. To read. To let God's word revive you. To tune your senses to His creation. To feel His presence in the present.

Into physical fitness? Work exercises into your daily domestic routine while you're waiting for time for a long walk or a bicycle ride. Involve your family in physical activity. Wish you were a teacher? Let your children be the fortunate ones whose education you enrich. Are you a closet homemaker who really relishes home keeping and cooking? Enjoy. And watch your family thrive too.

Crave time for a chosen interest or to discover a new one? What interests you? Are you trying to keep up with all the crafts your friends like? If you whittle away at yourself to suit all of their choices, you might end up a pile of shavings. What talents do you have you can develop? What can you dabble at now, without depreciating your family life, that will add dimensions later, and without making you feel like you're still just "whipping a tired horse?"

Women often "get away" in ways that refresh themselves, their homes, and those they give to: for example, sewing, painting, music, cooking, flower arranging, cake decorating, writing, photography. Flower gardening is fun for me, even in this small yard that fits my present strength, with benches worked in for resting. (My husband does the digging.) It's fun to plan the colors and arrangement of plants and shrubs, to nursery hop, plant, prune, and water, though sometimes I overdo it—like when the red geranium said to the pale pink petunia, "just tread water... she's going away for a week and you can dry out then."

Some think through the possibilities and choose to quilt, spin, weave, crochet, do needlepoint, cross stitch, embroider, make cards, curtains and cushions, or knit. Double knit afghans designed and knit by a beloved lady in our congregation still warm many of us. Through the years before her death, Frieda also blessed the lives of the children she taught in her fifth grade Bible class.

Many of you have also used spare, or created time, to teach children's classes; studying, preparing lessons, making visual aids, readying the classroom, even painting the walls. Some paint backdrops, scenes, or murals on them. Others have done hand work at home for teachers to use in the classroom. Many of you still do these things and more. As you take time, it's good to include activities such as these that expand you spiritually, and enrich the lives of others also. "A wise man's heart discerneth time and judgment" (Ecc 8.5).

NINE

Her husband is known in the gates
When he sitteth among the elders of the land.
She maketh linen garments and selleth them,
And delivereth girdles unto the merchant.

Verse 23 gives a second insight into the worthy woman's husband: the husband who trusts her with his heart (v 11), is trustworthy also, a man of integrity and reputation. He is "*known in the gates.*"

"A good name is rather to be chosen than great riches" (Prov 22.1). His "in the gates" good name is more valuable than riches, just as "her price is far above rubies." Her trustworthiness affects his reputation "in the gates." His "good name" shows he chooses to be worthy of her trust and honor.

Titus 2.6–8 teaches young men how to have "a good name." An opponent will have "no evil thing to say." First, "be soberminded." Then show "a pattern of good works, in doctrine showing integrity, reverence, sound speech, that cannot be condemned" (NKJV).

Daniel lived an example of excellence; a young man who "purposed in his heart that he would not defile himself with the king's dainties, and of the wine which he drank." Later, his "excellent spirit" distinguished him above nobility. "neither was there any error or fault found in him" (Dan 1.8; 6.3–4).

Young men can also look to the older men who are "temperate, grave, soberminded, sound in faith, in love, in patience" (Tit 2.1–2). Proverbs, such as the "my son" passages, increase a young man's wisdom. The Bible's complete teachings will make him complete, a man of "known in the gates" character. (2 Tim 3.16–17)

"In the Gates"

The gates, important to a city in ancient times, were often identified by name: "first gate," "corner gate," and "Benjamin's gate..." (Zech 14.10). They were sometimes named for the item sold near them: "fish gate" (Neh 3.3). Horses and other large animals entered through the "horse gate" (Neh 3.28, 2 Kgs 11.16). Gates were also used to explain locations: "In Jerusalem by the sheep gate" (John 5.2).

In the busy gateway setting of the ancient marketplace (see ch 5) the worthy woman's husband is recognized as one of the honorable men of the city "when he sitteth among the elders of the land."

Elders, a select group of godly men who acted as a city council, made themselves available "in the gates" for advice and witness. Boaz "went up to the gate, and sat him down there" and conducted his business before "ten men of the elders of the city" (Ruth 4.1–6). A person fleeing to a city of refuge could "stand at the entrance of the gate of the city, and declare his cause in the ears of the elders" (Josh 20.1–4).

Job gives eloquent insight into his activities "when he went forth to the gate unto the city" and "prepared his seat" in the broad place." "Men gave ear and waited, and kept silence for my counsel. I delivered the poor that cried, the fatherless also, that had none to help him. I caused the widow's heart to sing for joy." Clothed in righteousness and justice, Job was "eyes to the blind" and "feet... to the lame." He "searched out unknown needs. He plucked the prey out of the teeth of the unrighteous," and "smiled on them that had no confidence" (Job 29.7–22). This was not a wise words only position, but one of soul-rending responsibility.

Picture a city's elders sitting "in the broad place" of the street, their countenance befitting their wisdom and righteousness as they address the matters before them with integrity, insight, compassion, humility, and decisive courage. No nondescript, compla-cent men here. Or shallow-minded muscle men. Rather, there would be an aura of mental masculinity about them. "A wise man is strong; yea a man of knowledge increaseth might" (Prov 24.5).

New Testament Elders

Titus 1.7–9 gives the qualifications for elders in the New Tes-tament Church: "blameless, the husband of one wife, having chil-dren that believe, who are not accused of riot or unruly...for the bishop must be God's steward; not self-willed, not soon angry, no brawler, no striker, not greedy of filthy lucre; but given to hospi-tality, a lover of good, sober-minded, just, holy, self-controlled; holding to the faithful word which is according to the teaching, that he may be able both to exhort in the sound doctrine, and to convict the gainsayers." (See also 1 Tim 3.1–7)

Elders, or shepherds, have sobering responsibilities:

> Tend the flock of God which is among you, exercising the over-sight, not of constraint, but willingly, according to the will of God; nor yet for filthy lucre, but of a ready mind; neither as lording it over the charge allotted to you, but making yourselves examples to the flock. And when the chief shepherd shall be manifested, ye shall receive the crown of glory that fadeth not away. (1 Pet 5.2–4)

The "flock" has sobering responsibilities also: "Obey them that have the rule over you, and submit to them; for they watch in behalf of your souls, as they that shall give account; that they may do this with joy and not with grief" (Heb 13.17).

Worthy Men

"Come in; for thou art a worthy man." (Adonijah speaking to Jonathan; 1 Kgs 1.42)

God counted "known in the gates" men such as Noah, Abra-ham, Moses, Joshua, Jeremiah, Daniel, Ezekiel and Hezekiah worthy of responsibility, which each fulfilled in a worthy way. Joseph conducted himself worthily whether in a pit, palace, or prison. Mighty men such as David sinned mightily, but with heart-bending sorrow repented and regained spiritual stature. Job stayed faithful to God through grief and torment, though his also grieving, bitter wife told him to "renounce God and die," which would have rendered him worthless.

Through inspiration, a lineup of Old Testament men, along with many women, were counted worthy to be inducted into the Hebrews 11 Hall of Faith. Included are Abel, Enoch, Samuel, the prophets, and many more, "of whom the world was not worthy." (See also Worthy Man, Ezekiel.)

The many New Testament worthy men include the apostles, and Mark, Luke, Timothy, Titus, Epaphroditus, Gaius, Aquila, and other men mentioned in Romans 16.

Worthless Men

"A worthless person, a man of iniquity, is he that walketh with a perverse mouth; that winketh with his eyes, that speaketh with his feet, that makes signs with his fingers; in whose heart is perverseness, who deviseth evil continually, who soweth discord" (Prov 6–19)—not "in the gates" traits.

Though great in wealth, the evil, angry Nabal was considered worthless even among his own servants. They couldn't even discuss a concern with him. One said to Nabal's wife, Abigail, "He is such a worthless fellow that one cannot speak to him." Proverbs 22.24–25 says, "Make no friendship with a man who is given to anger; and with a wrathful man thou shalt not go: Lest thou learn his ways and get a snare to thy soul." (See also Worthy Woman: Abigail, end of chapter)

In contrast, the handsome Absalom was cunningly calm. He used his appeal in worthless ways: personal politics. He rose early and positioned himself by the gate to intercept any man coming to his father, David, for judgment, then feigning humility, told each one what he would do for him if only he were made judge.

He pretended empathy, took advantage of their vulnerability to manipulate their affections, "and stole the hearts of the men of Israel." His evil agenda and smooth, scheming ways led to his dishonorable death and broke his father's heart (2 Sam14:25; 15.2–6; 18.33)

Today as then, people often judge others by outward appearance. Many good men are handsome and strong, but a strong, handsome physique doesn't determine a man's worthiness. Proverbs 31 doesn't describe the worthy woman's husband's physical appearance, but as with his wife, the emphasis is on the inner "in the gates" qualities. God said of Eliab, "Do not look at his appearance or at his physical stature,… for the Lord does not see as man sees; for man looks on the outward appearance, but the Lord looks at the heart" (1 Sam 16.7 NKJV).

God has blessed me with a 53-year marriage (so far) to a "known in the gates" kind of husband, both in reputation and reality.

Wardrobes

Next the text brings us to the worthy woman's extra activities: "She maketh linen garments and selleth them. And delivereth girdles unto the merchants" (Prov 31.24).

Her trademark traits of integrity, industry, and ingenuity continue to thread their way through the sturdy fabric of her life, as demonstrated by the three verbs in this one verse. First, she "maketh linen garments."

The simply styled women's linen garments of her day included an under tunic, an outer tunic that covered from neck to ankle, and a belt, or girdle, that enabled them to gird their garments around the waist for quicker movement. They also gathered goods into the loose folds of their outer tunic, then tucked it under the belt forming a pouch, as women of more recent years used their aprons to tote vegetables from garden to kitchen.

The fuller, sometimes heavier, cloak or mantle could also be used to sleep in and for carrying things. Ruth slept in her mantle on the threshing floor in the evening, then used its folds to carry barley home to Naomi the next morning (Ruth 3.15).

A scarf-like headdress included a veil that covered the lower part of the female face. When Isaac's servant told the bride-to-be

Rebekah, it was Isaac, her intended, "walking in the field to meet them," she took her veil and covered herself" (Gen 24.65).

Included in the men's linen clothing was a wrap-around loin cloth, an under tunic and an over tunic that's length was suited to the wearer's activities. They also cinched their longer garments with girdles or belts to move quickly through narrow city streets, and for running. Elijah "girded up his loins, and ran before Ahab to the entrance of Jezreel" (1 Kgs 18.46).

A man's wide, all-in-one cloak or mantle also served as a blanket at night. "If you ever take your neighbor's garment as a pledge, you shall return it to him before the sun goes down; for that is his only covering... what will he sleep in?" (Exod 22.26–27 NKJV)

His headdress was often an oblong piece of fabric, folded to cover the forehead, come straight down at the sides, and form a V in the back. It was secured about the head by woolen threads.

Extra Activities

"And selleth them": The worthy woman sold her handmade garments to locals, caravan merchants passing her home, or merchants in the marketplace. She "delivereth" girdles unto the merchants.

She possibly bartered her quality handwork for merchandise such as the purple that was part of her wardrobe, though coins were in use. Perhaps some of the men who sat with her husband "in the gates" wore her workmanship purchased in the marketplace. Jeremiah is an example of a man sent to purchase a linen belt (Jer 13.1).

The worthy woman used her extra time, expertise, and quality linen to increase their assets, but her life didn't revolve around this sew-to-sell activity. It's listed last of her domestic pursuits, before going again to the inner aspects of herself and her family, and isn't singled out as a main source of satisfaction in the later account of her rewards. She keeps the big picture in view for next, verse 25 shows she focused her steady eye and positive perspective on the future.

Questions

1. From Proverbs 31.23, what does the worthy woman's husband's reputation "in the gates" say about him?

2. How would her strength of character and reputation affect his?

3. What are some qualities of worthy men mentioned in this chapter?

4. How did Absalom steal the hearts of the men of Israel?

5. From Proverbs 31.24 what qualities would help the worthy woman in her make-sell-and deliver endeavors?

Strength Training

1. Read Luke 1.5–24: Zecharias the priest and Elizabeth his wife.

2. Describe their lifestyle from verse 6.

3. Consider how we can use their example to strengthen ourselves spiritually.

4. Did their righteous life mean they would never face trials?

5. Today many men show strength as they live righteous lives of service to God, their families, and take a star-spangled stance for their country.

Worthy Man
Ezekiel

Ezekiel, an extraordinary envoy to the children of Israel during their 70 years of Babylonian captivity, was a priest and prophet of exceeding worth. God expected steadfast strength from him—and gave it. "The hand of the Lord was strong upon me" (Ezek 3.22 NKJV).

God sent him to the "rebellious nation," and the "impudent and stubborn children," to "give them warning" saying, "whether they hear or whether they refuse... yet they will know that a prophet has been among them. ...do not be afraid of their words or dismayed by their looks" (2.3–6).

Though in captivity, Ezekiel had a wife and a house (3.24).

We can imagine his godly wife waited for him and when he was able to come home, welcomed him, consoled him, and sent him out refreshed for his heart-wrenching responsibilities. To Ezekiel God called her "the desire of your eyes."

But soon he will be coming home to aloneness. No waiting arms—an empty house. For, "On this very day the king of Babylon started his siege against Jerusalem," God added the weight of grief to Ezekiel's already loaded shoulders saying, "behold, I take away from you the desire of your eyes with one stroke" (24.2, 15–16).

Now God, who strengthened him to "set [his] face toward the mountains of Israel" (6.2) will strengthen him to look the death of his beloved wife in the face and continue confronting the people. For Ezekiel, who has already experienced unusual suffering, will not be given time to grieve and must bear his sorrow alone, without showing emotion. "Yet you shall neither mourn nor weep, nor shall your tears run down. Sigh in silence, make no mourning for the dead" (24.15–17).

"So I spoke to the people in the morning: and at even my wife died; and I did in the morning as I was commanded" (v 18). Ezekiel did not lack love for his wife, but rather, because of God's commands, the urgency of His charge to him, and his intended example to Israel, he swallowed his grief and sighed in silence for the desire, or delight, of his eyes.

The "watchman" Ezekiel continues his difficult, God given mission to the idolatrous Israel. God rewards his service when the children of Israel listen to his words from God, repent, give up their idols, and a faithful remnant returns to Jerusalem. God chose Ezekiel for a certain purpose and he proved to be a man of unwavering faith, strength, and worth.

Facets
Spiritual Oneness

A special facet of a husband and wife's multi-faceted relationship is spiritual; two hearts joined in spiritual oneness with God, the one who joined you together as husband and wife.

It is a oneness worthy of developing—a oneness that is deepened and strengthened as you assemble together as individuals, and as husband and wife, with fellow Christians, to worship your creator. Praise, prayer, singing, and Bible study in the public assembly are an integral part of your lives, but worship doesn't stay there. It permeates your lives together. It enriches your relationship "in Christ," and with each other, to worship and study the Bible together at home. The two of you. Eyeball to eyeball. Heart to heart.

One young man steps naturally into his place as spiritual leader of their new home. Another grows into it slowly. Maybe he's shy. Or a new Christian. Or isn't interested. Maybe his father wasn't comfortable with Bible study or prayer in his home.

Encourage your husband. Perhaps in a time of a crisis or unexpected reprieve, ask him if he would lead the two of you in prayer—or initiate a positive discussion of the theme of a sermon or Bible class. Suggest studying a subject together at a specific time to help you learn and grow too.

Encourage him if he's asked to lead a public prayer, to lead a song, or give a talk. Allow him to learn. Making fun of, or ridiculing his efforts can slow his growth, discourage him from any attempt at a public part, and might humiliate him right on out the door.

A young woman sometimes blows opportunities to help her husband grow spiritually. Even one she has converted. Lost potential. Perhaps his soul. Rather than encouraging prayer, Bible study, "assembling together," and a close relationship with fellow Christians, they both become weaker, or unfaithful, because of worldliness, and/or out-of-whack priorities. This negligence also weakens or destroys their opportunities and responsibility to teach their children in the faith.

Even if your husband isn't a Christian, your daily behavior and sincere respect for him as your husband can win him to the word, and then you can begin your special spiritual journey together (1 Pet 3.1–2).

Abraham's obedience to God set an example to his wife, Sarah, as they left their homeland and together grew in faith on the trying trip to the promised land. The righteous Noah "walked with God" even though "the wickedness of man was great in the earth." He diligently obeyed "unto all that Jehovah commanded him" in such a way that his wife and three sons stood by him in faith through the long process of building the ark, and God brought them all to safety in it.

The New Testament also gives us inspiring examples, such as Zacharias and Elizabeth, a husband and wife who "were both righteous before God, walking in all the commandments and ordinances of the Lord blameless" (Luke 1.5–6).

Your service and salvation is individual (Phil 2.14). But cherish your spiritual oneness also. Make togetherness time to grow closer together spiritually. Go through life holding hearts and hands, "Hand In Hand With Jesus."

TEN

Strength and dignity are her clothing;
And she laugheth at the time to come.

"Strength and dignity" are the "fine linen and purple" of the worthy woman's inner attire and the foundation of her wardrobe. Her nobility of spirit casts a regal aura over such basics as kindness and commonsense. The classic qualities of "strength and dignity" are always in style and appropriate for every occasion. You won't find them on the discount rack of life. They are always "in the sight of God of great price."

"Strength and dignity" are not seasonal. These garments are never stored away. Just as the worthy woman readied their outer clothing for winter, she prepared her inner clothing for hard times. She was ready for the day her shoulders needed a sweater of strength thrown over them. "If you faint in the day of adversity, your strength is small" (Prov 24.10 NKJV).

There are countless women of all ages and circumstances who refuse to let their sweater of strength unravel during heartaches and hard times such as:

- The young woman who stands strong on her standards though classmates snub her into loneliness. One said, "This verse got me through high school."

- The strong single woman who, while longing for a husband,

patiently builds a life of noble character and purpose as she waits for one who is right for her.

- Those who lose all their possessions in natural disasters, but never lose their strength in the Lord.
- His strength bolsters the woman who faces down an addiction each time it turns up to tempt her-and wins.
- The homemaker who chooses to continue full time at her family-full life, though career-oriented friends and relatives tell her "There is more out there," stays strong.
- Strong-hearted wives prayerfully share in their husband's sacrifice as they and their children wait for his return from service for our country.
- Mothers who lovingly care for infants and children with special needs show admirable strength.
- Wives whose husbands desert them, but who do not desert the Lord, but rather rely on His strength through lonely struggles as they strive to raise their children to honor the Lord also.
- A double woven sweater of strength covers the shoulders of those whose infants or children's lives on earth are shortened by death.
- Wearing her sweater of strength, many an older woman tenderly tends to the husband she has known and loved for many years, though he no longer knows her.
- Strength fortifies the widow, young or old, who loses part of herself through the death of her husband, as she forces the motions of living until the ripping pain of separation dulls to an everyday throb.
- Many women face disease and death with strength enough for themselves and those who must see them suffer.
- Strong wives look to the Lord with faith and strengthen their husbands to do the same as they experience financial disaster.
- The elderly woman living out her life in a rest home, waiting patiently for her heavenly home, embodies "strength and dignity."

Strength is tightly woven into the many uniforms such as daughter, wife, mother, mother-in-law, daughter-in-law, grandmother, sister, sister-in-law, granddaughter, aunt, sister-in-Christ, friend, and neighbor, and unlike physical fabric, becomes stronger and sturdier with use. "Wherefore we faint not; but though our outward man is decaying, yet our inward man is renewed day by day" (2 Cor 4.16).

"Strength and dignity" don't depend on physical build or endurance. Inside many a physically fragile woman is a stout-hearted, ruddy cheeked, pioneer spirit of strength.

The Weak Woman Myth

Where did the myth of the weak woman come from? Not from the worthy woman of Proverbs 31. Her strength begins with the essence of the word "worthy" in verse 10 and permeates each quality through verse 31.

Throughout the Bible women showed strength in personal situations and impacted their society: women such as Ruth, who made hard decisions that honored God, and Esther who bravely did the right thing saying, "If I perish, I perish." Abigail's courage averted bloodshed for her household and affected David's future. Mary, the mother of Jesus, epitomized inner strength and dignity with her words and life.

Literary works have recognized the qualities of inner strength portrayed in the worthy woman as evidenced in William Wordsworth's poem about the perfect woman, "She Was a Phantom of Delight":

> And now I see with eye serene
> The very pulse of the machine;
> A being breathing thoughtful breath;
> A traveler between life and death;
> The reason firm, the temperate will,
> Endurance, foresight, strength, and skill.

Future Welcome Here

The worthy woman faces the future with a welcome sign. Her inner fashion philosophy not only clothes her with strength for the day, but confidence for the future: for "she laugheth at the time to come." She is not "afraid of evil tidings." Her sturdy inner wear assures her "heart is fixed, trusting in the Lord" (Psa 112.7).

Constant pursuit of excellence in all areas of life supports an optimistic outlook. The muddling through method leaves you open to discouragement. Tomorrow's challenges heaped on yesterday's unmet ones keep today's focus on the heap. The worthy woman has the telephoto lens on the future. She sees the long range goals which add importance to everyday duties. Even as she endures the pain and sorrow of the day, she "laugheth at the time to come."

"Laugheth" is "strength and dignity" with a cheerful countenance. "Laugheth" doesn't mean taking lightly the reality of the death or desertion of a loved one, or laughing off the discovery of a disease that projects you will live out your life in weakness and pain. It isn't false cheer at the knowledge your life savings have been stolen, or lost in an untimely investment. A worthy woman isn't jubilant every minute or gleeful over every drab detail, but even at the sobering news of death, disease, or misfortune, "strength and dignity" escort her into the future with cheer and confidence.

Tranquility with a Twinkle

"Life is too short not to have a smile on your face." Bert's life philosophy fueled her energy as we discovered the spiffy, reddish-haired, lanky lady walking to her apartment from a nearby nursing home where she had visited a friend and asked the receptionist if anyone else needed a visit. Then in her late eighties, her "I don't worry" faith in God had seen her through many challenges, including illness, the illness and death of her beloved husband, inspired her family and fellow Christians, and kept the Texas twinkle in her eyes.

Old age at its best is tranquility with a twinkle in its eye. A life well lived teaches the elderly person how to enjoy the now and happily prepare for the future. Some older women are happy. Some aren't. The difference doesn't depend on health or wealth. Most women don't joyfully leap into the arms of old age, but those with cheerful hearts gather gladness around them regardless of circumstances. Others let a stockpile of imagined miseries cause them to close up social shop and stagnate in self-pity rather than reaching out to clasp the hands that want to hold theirs.

At any age we can bully ourselves with bad attitudes and choke creative juices that could expand and energize our lives. Then, rather than laughing at "the time to come," we sentence ourselves to an "as is" life with no chance for improvement or enrichment.

When illness or accident cripples our plans we are frustrated, yet we can handicap ourselves with pessimism. Joseph could have gone from the pit to the self-pity pit. Instead, in each situation, he used his righteous disposition to overcome his position.

"Empty Nest"

One "time to come" many mothers dread is the "empty nest" stage. Some fear living a shell-like existence when the last child leaves home. Each does leave a special space, but does the worthy woman seem likely to become an empty shell?

Will the capabilities and inner resources you develop by living the life of a godly woman, wife, and mother abruptly become useless? Will the qualities, talents, and insights gained as a result of raising children go out the door with them? Does the attitude of excellence and willing contribution to the welfare of others become worthless? When you put the seashell of memory to your mind's ear, it echoes back the love, wisdom, and experience that have settled on the sands of your life, ready to warm others.

As older women you can feel satisfaction in your blessings and accomplishments and enjoy setting new goals. You have more freedom to give more freely to others. You are more often able to adjust your activities to present levels of health and work to improve it. And what better time to pursue spiritual development? Though grown up we are never spiritually "full grown."

Think about your assets and abilities. Your value. You may enter the empty nest stage feeling like an empty shell but, like the weather-worn pen shell, inside you are mother of pearl.

Reunited

The empty nest stage brings special benefits, such as more time to enjoy your husband; to savor, and invigorate your relationship. To think anew about ways to "do him good." To continue the knowing and growing process of chapter two.

Maybe it's also time to think toward a realistic and rewarding retirement. Some husbands and wives just wake up "retired."
Soon they realize that his dream of being permanently propped
up against a tree with his fishing line dangling in a wooded stream,
and hers of being permanently parked at Mall of America might
need some adjusting. Or, she's envisioning tweaking their budget
to permit plane trips to their out of state children, and he's out
test-driving Harley Davidsons.

As part of their increased together time before and after retirement many plan to continue their lifetime of service to others and
to the Lord; even increasing the time and resources they share.
They may downsize their home, but not their service.

An older wife often determines to enjoy her husband while she
still has him rather than spending so much time in classes and jobs
preparing for widowhood that she's always gone before he's gone.

Sadly, some men find themselves alone, deserted by wives
who, as Lot's wife, looked back into the world and denounced
"all the days of his life." Wives might more easily influence their
husbands toward evil when they are older and more vulnerable.
Solomon's wives turned his heart away from God "when he was
old" (1 Kgs 11.4).

A long, strong marriage reaps many blessings. Those blessed
with grandchildren and great-grandchildren enjoy their special-
ness, and the wonder of watching their lives and adding fun and
value to them, as they enrich and enliven yours; plus, they keep you
on your mental toes—like when a young southern granddaughter
sits there, butterfly pretty with sweetness to spare, throwing us off
guard, just before she wallops Grandpa and me in a board game.

Sometimes they brighten your fingernails too, and impress
you with their kindness, as when our oldest granddaughter and
I sat together at a salon letting our nails dry. When she learned
this treat during my visit was my first ever manicure, she sweetly
resisted saying my nails looked it. The younger grand girls and
boys could care less about nails as we play and plant in the not
so secret garden.

Alone

A wife misses her mate and longs to share special times with him long after he is gone. With sorrow-laden "strength and dignity" she learns again to laugh "at the time to come" as she faces the challenges each lonely new day brings. I've heard widows, such as my sister say "I'm trying to live a life that will honor him, even though he's gone." One afternoon she came home to the shock of finding her 68 year-old husband dead of a heart attack at his computer. Still, she continued her faithful worship and Bible class attendance, and personal Bible studies. Soon, though inwardly sorrowful, and struggling with painful knee problems, she was back at preparing food for the sick and grieving, sending encouraging cards, and teaching a children's Bible class.

All ages of women of scary circumstances shoulder on into the future with confidence, strengthened by their faith in God. Their worries take wings as they say with David, "I have set the Lord always before me; Because He is at my right hand I shall not be moved. Therefore, my heart is glad, and my glory rejoices" (Psa 16.8). Philippians 4.4–9 also helps one rejoice and forbear. (See ch 4.)

Many elderly ladies continue blessing others with their words, enriched by scripture, prayer, and songs, in their homes, and even in their convalescent homes, seeming to say with the Psalmist, "Yea, even when I am old and grey-headed, O God, forsake me not, until I have declared thy strength unto the next generation, Thy might to everyone who is to come" (Psa 1.18). Envision an elderly lady, perhaps with a shawl around her frail, but spiritually strong shoulders, her Bible in her lap, with young women and children gathered around her, still declaring His strength and His might to the young, so that one day they too may "laugh at the time to come."

Even winter-worn elderly women who are past the time of purposeful influence, often lift others through a memory their gesture or expression invokes, a smile, or an unexpected song:

Hattie

At 6:45 AM Hattie sat in her wheelchair in the darkened nursing home hallway. The tall Texan's white hair was brushed back from her strong cheekbones and hung in a thick braid down the back of her purple sweatshirt. Her head was bowed, her eyes closed, and her fingers poised in a prayer-like position on her chin. Al and I moved quietly past her to a room across the hall and stood at his mother's bedside where she lay near death.

Suddenly, "There's a beautiful place called heaven, it is hidden above the bright blue..." We looked to the doorway where Hattie, sleeping beauty now turned songstress, had wheeled herself. "Where the good, who from earth ties are riven, live and love an eternity thru. Above the bright blue, the beautiful blue," Hattie continued in her deep, ninety-five-year-old voice. "Jesus is waiting for me and for you." Tears blurred our eyes as we stood before this privileged recital. "Heaven is there, not far from our sight, Beautiful city of light." From nearly a century of heaven-bound songs stored in her heart, Hattie had lifted our hearts with this touching scene of two dear Christian ladies, one singing to the other who could not speak, as they "laughed at the time to come."

Questions

1. What are some circumstances or times of life that strain your strength?

2. What helped, or is helping, you through them?

3. How can this experience help you "laugh at the time to come"?

Strength Training

1. Choose a Bible woman who is an example of "strength and dignity" to you and write a paragraph or more explaining why.

2. How can you emulate those qualities?

Worthy Woman
Jochebed

Egypt's new king had a problem: "The people of the children of Israel are more and mightier than we." Fear of their possible power in confrontation caused him to devise evil plans to weaken and control them. "Therefore they set taskmasters over them to afflict them with their burdens." "But the more they afflicted them, the more they multiplied and grew." So the Egyptians made the lives of the Israelites "bitter with hard bondage-in mortar, in brick, and in all manner of service in the field."

Next, the king of Egypt told the midwives who helped the Hebrew woman give birth, to kill their baby sons. "But the midwives feared God" and did not obey the king's command. They explained to Pharaoh that the Hebrew women gave birth quickly before the midwives could get there.

Again King Pharaoh chose murder as a control tactic. He commanded all his people, saying, "Every son who is born, you shall cast into the river." Though the king of Egypt desperately attempted to control the Hebrew population, a man of the house of Levi and his wife Jochebed, "were not afraid of the king's commandment." By faith they decided to hide their baby son.

After Jochebed decided "she could no longer hide him," strengthened by her faith in God and her love for her baby son, she took a basket made of bulrushes, water-proofed it with pitch, "put the child in it, and laid it in the reeds by the river's bank." Then she stationed his sister Miriam, "afar off" so they would know what happened to him.

One day Pharaoh's daughter saw the basket and told her maidens to bring it to her. When she opened it "behold, the baby wept. And she had compassion on him, and said, 'This is one of the Hebrew's children.'" Then Miriam, with an alertness and composure belieing her young years, honed by helping her mother care for and quiet her baby brother during his first months of hiding, said to Pharaoh's daughter, "Shall I go and call a nurse for you from the Hebrew women, that she may nurse the child for you?" Imagine Miriam's excitement as she ran to tell her mother, and their tearful hugs at the joyous news that their baby would be spared.

Next, her strength and dignity befitting a child of the King, Jochebed went to meet the daughter of the king of Egypt. The princess approved her and said, "Take this child away and nurse him for me and I will give you your wages." Jochebed's faith was rewarded far beyond the pay from Pharaoh's daughter, as she loved and taught their son for part of his young years.

Then, knowing God had once brought him from the basket of bulrushes back into her arms must have strengthened her as she returned him to Pharaoh's daughter who claimed him as her son, and named him Moses. Though she acted as his mother, "by faith, Moses, when he was grown up, refused to be called the son of Pharaoh's daughter." Those recorded as "his parents" in Hebrews 11.23, were Amram, and the worthy woman Jochebed (Num 26.59; Exod 1.8–2.10)

Facets
Sorrow–Mysterious Magnet?

What is there about sorrow that makes one want to slow down, back up, and walk barefoot through it, and why do we trip lightly over joy with merely a backward glance? Why do we hug sorrow to us, squeezing tightly, savoring every drop of anguish, and why do we so soon release joy with undeserved frigidity?

Oh, there are accepted times of happiness, such as the thrill of the knowledge of our first true love, when a woman is obviously and radiantly with child, or the joyous reunion with loved ones after a long separation. These are traditional times to laugh and dream, feeling as if no one else could possibly be so happy.

But what of the delicious little thrilling moments we so hastily pass by? Why isn't the opposite true? Shouldn't it be so to pause, turn and savor that exquisite rosebud, to commit to memory that impish, unphotographical little expression, to take time to count every daffodil tip peeping through the snow, to reflect upon the special beauty of an act of unselfishness, or to watch the sunset on a snow covered mountain through each color change from pink to purple to blue?

Are we so morbid we would rather spend ten minutes thinking and talking of a recent account of horror, and ten seconds watching the iridescent wonder of dew sparkling on the grass? Did the coffee we drank with the morning paper awaken our eyes to the dew? What will awaken our hearts, our very souls, to the glories around us; our imaginations to the wonders of this giant top we are so slowly, surely spinning on at this very moment, never wavering nor toppling as would a miniature manmade replica?

What will cause us to thirst to drink in the beauties around us? Is God saddened that we are so indifferent to the magnificence that surrounds us while we dwell on what has been taken away? Do we cling to sorrow when "in thy presence is fullness of joy" (Psa 16.11)? Do we forget that it is written in the word of the One who can wipe away all tears that "weeping may tarry for the night but joy cometh in the morning" (Psa 30.5)?

Our alert imaginations can move appreciatively from the mental vision of the nine planets precisely placed, to the tiny bees in their hive, also a demonstration of precision. At the very least an hour could be filled in a park or garden entranced with the shades, blends, and hues of color, only to begin anew if shapes, textures, and sizes were considered.

Can we look God's glories in the face and reflect gloom? Would we revel in illness rather than improvement? Should we not dismiss sadness in search of song? Is joy really so elusive or do we make easy her escape? Do we reject God's gracious offers of release (Psa 34.18–19; Phil 4.4–7)?

The refreshment of a true vacation cannot equal the invigorating, renewing, and awakening that comes from struggling with a darkness within your own inner being and coming up not only victorious, but strengthened by the struggle (Rom 5.3).

Sorrow draws you down into its mocking, echoing pit, while joy lifts you up as with the caress of an omnipotent hand. Let us not be bound to misfortune by a web of bitterness, but snip the subtle, smothering thread, and arise, and let that sunshiny morning feeling fill our souls. "Yea, happy is the people whose God is Jehovah" (Psa 144.15).

Darlene Craig
Vanguard Magazine
1975

ELEVEN

She openeth her mouth with wisdom,
And the law of kindness is on her tongue.

On May 18, 1980 Mt. St. Helens erupted. At 8:32 AM, the now famous lady spoke in awesome tones. Fuming and steaming she warmed to the momentous event with a few warning rumbles. Then, with a blast that flattened forests, buried sparkling streams, suffocated rabbits and raccoons, frightened deer into statue-like figures, smothered stranded people, and destroyed homes, she made known her violent nature.

Those of us far enough away from our noisy Washington neighbor to escape direct devastation felt the gritty, grey ash turn our fresh, Oregon air into a heavy, stinging substance as it settled in a gloomy fog on people and property.

Just as Mt. St. Helens has dangerous volcanic tendencies, some wives and mothers are prone to volatile outbursts. Some are unpredictable. Others erupt at regular intervals. Each day the wary household waits for the lady of the house to blast off. Then she speaks as did the mountain, in fuming fury, spewing hot, stinging air that sends the family into hiding as they wait for the most recent eruption to fizzle out. Once the pent up pressure is released, the fallout of grey gloom, like the dread volcanic ash, settles over the victims, leaving an oppressive layer of emotional sludge in its wake.

Proverbs 30.21–23 forecasts a volcanic woman's earth-shaking effect on a marriage. One of four things listed that causes the earth to tremble is "an odious woman when she is married" (NKJV gives "hateful" for "odious").

Some use their explosive nature as did the wolf in "The Three Little Pigs," threatening "If I don't get my way, I'll huff and I'll puff and I'll blow your house in." Sadly, some do blow their homes apart in this manner. In contrast, the "far above rubies" woman of Proverbs 31.26 "openeth her mouth with wisdom" that is "more precious than rubies" (Prov 3.15). "Yea, the price of wisdom is above rubies" (Job 28.18).

Where can we get wisdom? "For the Lord gives wisdom…He stores up sound wisdom for the upright" (Prov 2.6–7). "But if any of you lacks wisdom let him ask of God…" (Jas 1.5). James 3.17 gives eight ways to identify God's wisdom: "The wisdom that is from above is first pure, then peaceable, gentle, willing to yield, full of mercy and good fruits, without partiality, without hypocrisy…"

Slow to Speak

"Wisdom is knowing when to speak your mind, and when to mind your speech," a wise person once said. Ecclesiastes 3.7 says there is "a time to keep silence and a time to speak." James 1.19 cautions, "be swift to hear, slow to speak." "The heart of the righteous studies how to answer" (Prov 15.28 NKJV). Prepare your heart—prepare your answer. The scriptures' timeless advice for timely speech applies to private conversation, and public comment. Will our words lift someone up, or cause them to give up? Are they kind? Are they circumspect? "He that restrains his lips is wise" (Prov 10.19 NKJV). (See Worthy Woman, Abigail at the end of the chapter for an example of a woman of wise words.)

Foolish Words

"The lips of the wise disperse knowledge; But the heart of the foolish doeth not so" (Prov 15.7). Wise words from the wise woman's lips helped her do her husband "good and not evil," whereas, when Job lost his possessions, then his children, and now sat in the ashes so covered with boils that his friends did not recognize him, his bitter grieving wife mocked him with challenging, blasphemous words: "Do you still hold fast to your integrity? Curse God and die!"

Her foolish words, heaped on the coals of his misery, could have caused him to give up on himself, and God. Instead, Job rebuked her saying, "You speak as one of the foolish women speaks. Shall we indeed accept good from God, and shall we not accept adversity?" Job's wife scorned and belittled him when he most needed her. Yet, "In all this Job did not sin with his lips" (Job 2.7–10, NKJV).

WIWO

GIGO—the computer acronym meaning Garbage in, Garbage Out—is also true of our inner computers: Garbage In, Garbage Out. Mixing garbage with wisdom garbles mind and spirit. "Out of the same mouth proceed blessing and cursing. My brethren, these things ought not to be so. Does a spring send forth fresh water and bitter from the same opening?" (Jas 3.10, 11, NKJV). "The heart of the wise teaches his mouth" (Prov 16.23, NKJV). And turning it around, "The mouth of the righteous brings forth wisdom" (Prov 10.31, NKJV). WIWO: Wisdom In, Wisdom Out.

Lovely looking women spoil the image they work to create when garbage can words spill over their carefully lacquered lips. You cringe and resist the impulse to impale a thesaurus on the offensive tongue. "Let no corrupt speech proceed out of your mouth" (Eph 4.29).

Movies and television programs are known to increasingly contain swear words and outright obscene language. Some newscasters and talk show hosts, not just ill-spoken guests, use foul language. A pretty, young news analyst defended the use of swear words on the public networks, indiscreetly wasting her potential influence for good on this topic in this arena. "As a ring of gold in a swine's snout, so is a fair woman without discretion" (Prov 11.22).

Many unwisely use God's holy name as if it were an exclamation point. "You shall not take the name of the Lord your God in vain; for the Lord will not hold him guiltless who takes His name in vain" (Exod 20.7 NKJV). Often, perhaps without realizing it, people use sound-like substitutes for God, Jesus, and Lord. Some sling slang words that sound too close for comfort to their cuss word cousins. The Proverbs 31 woman "openeth her mouth with wisdom" (Prov 31.26).

Laying Down the Law

The last part of verse 26 shows the worthy woman laid down the law for her tongue in her heart. "The law of kindness is on her tongue." Kindness ruled. "Whoever guards his mouth and tongue, keeps his soul from troubles" (Prov 21.23 NKJV).

Humans crave kindness. Shakespeare said "kindness in women, not their beauteous looks shall win my heart." Kindness includes appreciation and admiration. Children thrive on them. They do wonders for wives. Husbands need them too.

A friend whose wife died, said "It helped so much after she died to walk through the house and remember kind words and happy times." If we died today how would our husband walk through the house? Remembering good times, kind words? Or "Ah, my favorite chair. Right where I was sitting when she told me what a bum I was." Or "Oh that kitchen table. We had some of our best fights there."

Kind words are crucial to a loving, lasting marriage. Just as high tide washes away love notes and sand castles, high temper words can erase tender times, and undo I Do's.

Criticism KOs Kindness

"A gentle tongue is a tree of life; But perverseness therein is a breaking of the spirit" (Prov 15.4). Criticism knocks out kindness. If your husband seems unloving, uncooperative, defensive, or lazy, criticism can be the culprit. It can be spoken or inferred. A know it all attitude affects his. If he has to do everything your way, he starts thinking "No way." He's more likely to do his part to lighten your load or just to be with you, than because "You better get that done or else," with the finish followed by "Can't you do anything right?"

Criticism through constant comparison with other men, whether a public figure, a best friend's husband, a brother, or your father, stifles rather than motivates your husband. Sometimes a wife treats her husband like a boy. If she wants a man's opinion, she asks her father. A father's insight can be helpful to both, but he didn't bring to his marriage all the wisdom and expertise he might have as an older husband. The young husband deserves the opportunity to learn to love and lead in an encouraging atmosphere. The kind worded woman of Proverbs 31.26 laid down the law to her tongue, not her husband.

Rat-a-Tat-Tongue

Some older couples communicate by nagging and picking at each other, most likely a habit they picked up in their younger years and let stick like lint to an old pair of socks.

Wives of any age can get in the habit of handling their husband with an ever-ready rat-a-tat tongue. "Heaviness in the heart of a man maketh it stoop; But a good word maketh it glad" (Prov 12.25). For stoop the NKJV says "causes depression." Bitter, abusive words beat down rather than inspire to rise to daily challenges.

Proverbs 21.19 says "Better to dwell in the wilderness than with a contentious and angry woman" (NKJV). A combative black starling reminded me of this verse as it peck-peck-pecked at the back of a blue heron walking around a small pond, finally provoking it away from its peaceful pond setting. Then, still not satisfied at the heron's resigned departure, the starling flew above it, pecking at his back as he flew out of sight.

"Do Your Own Business"

When kindness "rules the tongue" gossip is ruled out. First Thessalonians 4.11 instructs: "study to be quiet, and to do your business, and to work willingly with your hands." Doing "your own business" keeps you from minding the business of others. Young widows were urged to marry, lest they "learn also to be idle, going about from house to house, and not only idle, but tattlers also and busybodies, speaking things which they ought not"

(1 Tim 5.13). Today's technology such as the telephone, E-mail, Facebook, and text messaging make it easy for any age to go from "house to house" without leaving home.

Many earn their livelihood making other people's business their business. These are the gossip-mongers who suck up questionable information and spit out the evil concoction in print. They prey on hurting people, making the tragedies, mistakes, and losses of others their personal gain. They dig up facts and fiction through bribe or boldness and scoop it out to ready readers. "An ungodly man digs up evil" (Prov 16.27 NKJV).

It seems despicable for a worldly person to earn his living digging up malicious morsels and relaying the embellished bits to those willing to pay for, or listen to such. But is the "law of kindness" on the tongue of the Christian who, on a smaller, seemingly more innocent scale, gathers questionable information and furnishes it to fellow Christians for free?

This gives a false sense of popularity not truly enjoyed by the chief go-between gossip or admired by those who become involved in the contention it stirs up. "A whisperer separates the best of friends" (Prov 16.28). "The north wind brings forth rain; And a backbiting tongue an angry countenance" (Prov 25.23), whereas "wisdom speaks of excellent things" (Prov 8.6, NKJV).

Archery

"Whoever spreads slander is a fool" (Prov 10.18 NASB). Older women are told to be "not slanderers," in Titus 2.3. The NASB says "malicious gossips." Again, in 1 Timothy 3.11 "women in like manner must be "not slanderers." Slander includes telling untruths, devastating to a person's reputation. So it is that the sin of lying enters into gossip.

Jeremiah 9.3–8 shows characteristics of slander: "Like their bow they have bent their tongues for lies. And every neighbor will walk with slanderers... will deceive his neighbor, and will not speak the truth; they have taught their tongue to speak lies. ...Their tongue is an arrow shot out; it speaks deceit: One speaks peaceably to his neighbor with his mouth, but in his heart he lies in wait" (NKJV).

In Psalm 28.3 David cried unto the Lord that he not be taken away with those who "speak peace with their neighbors, but evil is in their hearts." Is evil in the heart today when one speaks kindness intended for evil? Or speaks kindly to friends, but cruelly to others? Christ, our example of the perfect use of mouth and tongue "did not sin, neither was guile found in his mouth: Who, when he was reviled, reviled not again; when he suffered, threatened not..." (1 Pet 2.23).

Paul wanted even personal disagreements to be resolved. In Philippians 4.2–3 he exhorts Euodia and Syntyche to face their friction and "become like-minded," rather than letting their differences diminish their work for the Lord. (See Euodia and Syntyche, end of chapter)

Scripture addresses all possibilities of the tongue for good or evil. I've attempted to touch on some of them in this and other chapters. For many years I have been blessed to be in a congregation where women have worked, and played at having the loving sisterly relationship discussed in the Networking section of Chapter 3. Wise words are an integral part of this special relationship, that we may "love life, and see good days" (1 Pet 3.10).

Let us pray with the Psalmist, "Set a guard, O Lord, over my mouth; keep watch over the door of my lips" (Psa 141.3), that we may open our mouths with wisdom and keep the law of kindness on our tongues.

Questions

1. What are we not to be like? (Psa 32.9 NKJV) Instead, wisdom cries out by the gates to "be of an understanding heart" (Prov 8.5).

2. Who first felt the effects of the worthy woman's wisdom and kindness?

3. From the WIWO section find three scriptures that show the heart's part in what our mouth and tongue disperse.

4. How can our self-talk influence how we talk to others?

Strength Training

1. Our Strength Training Exercise begins with balance. What is essential to good balance in life? (Prov 3.21–23; 4.11–13)

2. When is archery not a good exercise? (Jer 9.3, 8)

3. From Proverbs 6.12–14, who makes a poor walking companion?

4. What are six instructions regarding the path of the wicked? (Prov 4.14–15)

5. Describe the path of the righteous. (Prov 4.18)

6. Make this a wise words week. Meditate on Bible verses about the tongue: Make thoughts and words match. (Psa 19.14; 1 Pet 3.10)

Worthy Woman
Abigail

"The excellency of knowledge is, that wisdom preserveth the life of him that hath it" (Ecc 7.12). Abigail's wisdom proved to be a life preserver for her household (1 Sam 25.1–38).

Abigail was a woman of "good understanding, and of a beautiful countenance." Her husband, Nabal, was "churlish and evil." When Nabal's shepherds herded his many sheep in the Wilderness of Paran, David and his men were "a wall unto them both by night and day," protecting them from being harmed or robbed.

When David and his men needed food and water, he sent ten men to the wealthy Nabal who was celebrating with a sheep-shearing feast. The ten greeted Nabal in peace, recounted their protective care of Nabal's men, and requested food and water in David's name.

Nabal scoffed. "Who is David?" David who? Then he berated them with a selfish "I," "my," "my," "I," "my" account of his own abundant supplies. The ten left and reported to David.

Shortly, one of Nabal's servants, knowing Nabal to be a "worthless fellow, that one cannot speak to," told Abigail about David's protection of Nabal's men, David's request and Nabal's rebuff. Meanwhile, David's 400 armed men headed their way to kill all males in Nabal's household for revenge.

Abigail and some male servants quickly loaded donkeys with food and other peace-offerings and left to meet David. When David and his armed men came down the mountain toward her, the brave Abigail fell at his feet with humble "My Lord," "Your handmaid" greetings. She apologized for her husband's foolish words, spoke to David of his soul relationship with the living God, gave God the credit for saving David from this "blood guiltiness," and offered her generous gifts.

Abigail further inspired David with a reminder of all the good God would do in his lifetime and warned that this planned bloodshed would one day bring him grief. She did not manipulate David, but rather spoke wise words that changed his heart. David blessed God, then Abigail saying "blessed be thy discretion." He realized God had brought this lovely woman whose wise words calmed him and halted his aggressive plans.

She returned home and found Nabal feasting like a king and drunk. Again using discretion, she waited until morning "when the wine was gone out of Nabal," then told him what had almost happened. Her report caused a stroke-like reaction in Nabal's body. Days later, God smote him dead.

Nabal's arrogant, foolish words had nearly destroyed lives, but Abigail spoke as a worthy woman, wise, peace-making words that preserved the lives of those in her household. "In the lips of him who has discernment, wisdom is found" (Prov 13.10).

Facets
Euodia And Syntyche

"I exhort Euodia, and I exhort Syntyche…." Paul exhorts these two women by name—individually, and equally. "Be of the same mind in the Lord" (Phil 4.2). Why did they need this exhortation? Were disagreements related to the work distracting them from their "in the gospel" goals? A personality clash? Competition over who had done the most for the longest? What was their problem?

It's none of our business. Paul tells us what we need to know. The details were evidently not meant for our minds, but "being of the same mind" was. So let's calm our curiosity and consider what he does, through the Holy Spirit, reveal.

Being "of the same mind" was important to Paul. He even urged another fellow-worker to help. Was his "true yoke-fellow" hesitant to get between two at-odds women? We only know Paul urged him to "help these women."

Philippians 1.27 helps us understand "of the same mind." "Only let your manner of life be worthy of the gospel of Christ; ... that ye stand fast in one spirit, with one soul striving for the faith of the gospel." Paul was joyful when the Philippian Christians were "of the same mind," and described it in four different ways: "be of the same mind, having the same love, being of one accord, of one mind" (Phil 2.2).

He stresses unselfishness and humility to them and gives the ultimate example: "Have this mind in you, which was also in Christ Jesus." Incomprehensible humility. Supreme unselfishness (vv 5–8).

In verses 19–23 Paul praises his unselfish, "like-minded" fellow-servant Timothy, and tells them to receive and show honor to a courageous "fellow worker," Epaphroditus.

He considers Euodia and Syntyche fellow workers with such, and "Clement also, and the rest of my fellow workers, whose names are in the book of life," even though these spiritually minded, hard-working women weren't perfect. Neither are we. We might even need to be exhorted. But, as we always strive to be spiritually mature (3.15), and "of the same mind in the Lord," we can rejoice with fellow Christians, knowing our "names are in the book of life."

TWELVE

She looketh well to the ways of her household,
And eateth not the bread of idleness.

A pretty, twelve-year-old girl is being made up for a modeling session with a photographer. Her eyelashes thicken and darken. Her once innocent eyes now look sultry and worldly wise. Her pale, sweet mouth becomes dark and sensual. Her school-girl clothes have been exchanged for a shiny, black evening dress designed to expose what her blouse had modestly covered. She lies stomach down on a table. Her long hair is fluffed over her bare shoulder and her pre-teen body is coaxed into the seductive pose of a sophisticated woman of the world.

The host for the TV documentary questions her mother concerning the effect this environment and being portrayed in this manner in slick magazines might have on her daughter. The girl's mother sees no harm in it and expects no harmful effects.

It's the photographer who expresses concern in answer to the interviewer's questions. He has seen the soft, happy innocence of young models used in this way become hardened and saddened. Some modeled an arrogant attitude. Some turned to drugs. He said, "Her mother isn't aware of its effect on her." How sad. The photographer was more aware than her mother of the dangers to her daughter. True, he was seeing through the focused eyes of an experienced photographer, but she had the vantage point of motherhood—and mothers must be aware.

Aware means to be vigilant, informed, on one's guard. Vincent's New Testament Word Study gives "guardian" or "guard" for "keepers at home" (Tit 2.5). Part of the mother's work is to keep a moral and spiritual watch over her children: "Be sober, be vigilant: your adversary the devil, walks about, as a roaring lion seeking whom he may devour" (1 Pet 5.8 NKJV).

"My being gone is good for my children" says a mother of preteens. "It teaches them to look out for themselves." Proverbs 13.27 shows the worthy woman looking out for her children. Looking out for your children doesn't mean waiting on them hand and foot, but rather, directing their footsteps. "A child left to himself brings shame to his mother" (Prov 29.15 NKJV).

The worthy woman looks "well to the ways of her household." This is an all around, in-depth, pay attention process involving love, wisdom, work, persistence, and common sense. It isn't surface supervision. A mother has the zoom lens focused on her family, giving her a close-up view with a long-range eternal perspective.

Teaching Technique

Read the vigilance and teaching expected from parents under Old Testament law: "Only take heed to yourself, and diligently keep yourself, lest you forget the things your eyes have seen and lest they depart from your heart all the days of your life. And teach them to your children and your grandchildren" (Deut 4.9 NKJV).

Deuteronomy 31.12 details the public part of their teaching process: "Gather the people together, men, and women, and little ones, and the stranger… that they may hear and that they may learn to fear the Lord your God and carefully observe all the words of this law, and that their children who have not known it may hear and learn to fear the Lord your God and carefully observe all the words of this law."

Deuteronomy 6.4–7, a favorite of many mothers, gives both specific and practical instructions: "Hear O Israel: The Lord our God, the Lord is one: You shall love the Lord your God with all your heart, with all your soul, and with all your strength. And these words which I command you today shall be in your heart.

You shall teach them diligently to your children, and shall talk of them when you sit in your house, when you walk by the way, when you lie down, and when you rise up" (NKJV).

One evening while in the living room reading their Bible story to the three younger boys, one wrote "I LOVE GOD" in large letters in his Bible with his yellow highlighter, highlighting to me the impression God's word was making on his young heart.

Heart to Heart

Second Timothy 1.5 gives an excellent example of generational heart to heart teaching. Paul, speaking to Timothy, says, "When I call to remembrance the genuine faith that is in you, which dwelt first in your grandmother Lois and your mother Eunice, and I am persuaded in you also" (NKJV). The faith-full heart of Grandmother Lois planted faith in the heart of her daughter Eunice.

Second Timothy 3.14–15 shows Timothy's part in this ongoing process: "But you must continue in the things which you have learned and been assured of, knowing from whom you learned them, and that from childhood you have known the Holy Scriptures, which are able to make you wise unto salvation through faith which is in Christ Jesus." Verses 16 and 17 show the life and soul spanning scope of the "Holy Scriptures" Timothy learned in this heart to heart process.

A Mother's Heart

"A mother's heart is a child's schoolroom." Henry Ward Beecher authored this thought provoking saying. The worthy woman's watchful heart was indeed a suitable setting for instructing and guiding her children.

Mary, the mother of Jesus, had a watchful, thoughtful heart. After the birth of Jesus, and the visit by the shepherds, "Mary kept all these sayings, pondering them in her heart" (Luke 2.19). After hearing his explanation when, at age 12, Joseph and Mary found Jesus in the temple learning and asking questions, "his mother kept all these sayings in her heart" (Luke 2.51).

She watched and weighed the events involving their child and held them in her motherly heart. "Jesus advanced in wisdom and stature, and in favor with God and man" (Luke 2.52). (See Worthy Women—Mary and Elizabeth—end of chapter).

Spiritual Starter Dough

A mother's heart can also tutor a child to its destruction. "As is the mother, so is the daughter." In this allegory Jerusalem is rebuked with the words, "You are your mother's daughter, loathing husband and children" (Ezek 16.44–45 NKJV).

Within the mother's heart lies the spiritual starter dough for her children. Her heart's stirrings bubble down through the generations producing good or evil. Jezebel's heart activated evil in the hearts of her children and husband, already an evil activist. "But there was none like unto Ahab, who did sell himself to do that which was evil in the sight of Jehovah, whom Jezebel his wife stirred up" (1 Kgs 21.25). As if there wasn't enough evil brewing in the diabolical mind of her husband Ahab, Jezebel stoked the fires, furthering their evil influence and sending it seething through the lives of their children.

Their son Ahaziah "did that which was evil in the sight of Jehovah, and walked in the way of his mother" (1 Kgs 22.51). Jehu said to Joram, son of Jezebel, "What peace, so long as the harlotries of your mother Jezebel and her witchcraft are so many?" (2 Kgs 9.22 NKJV).

Just as Jezebel incited her husband Ahab to even more evil, her daughter Athaliah stirred the evil passions of her husband, King Jehoram, who "walked in the way of the kings of Israel, as did the house of Ahab, for he had the daughter of Ahab to wife" (2 Kgs 8.18).

She is described as "that wicked woman…" Her sons, Jezebel's grandsons, "had broken up the house of God; and also all the dedicated things… did they bestow upon the Baalim" (2 Chron 24.7). Athaliah's son Ahaziah "walked in the ways of the house of Ahab; for his mother was his counselor to do wickedly" (2 Chron 22.1–4). Athaliah not only counseled her children and grandchildren to spiritual destruction, she killed her own grandchildren, the great-grandchildren of Jezebel (2 Chron 22.10–12).

In contrast, a worthy woman's lifetime of doing her husband "good and not evil," and looking "well to the ways of her household," profoundly affects their lives for good. She exemplifies the wise woman who "builds her house," and Jezebel, the "foolish woman who "pulls it down with her own hands" (Prov 14.1 NKJV).

Fathers Too

Dad's aren't just bench sitters or ball game buddies. They are major leaguers in the game plan for their children's lives. Scriptures cited earlier show the father's responsibility and influence on their children's character. Proverbs 1.8 and 6.20 also show that father and mother each have a role in teaching their children.

New Testament scripture exhorts: "Fathers, provoke not your children to wrath, but nurture them in the chastening and admonition of the Lord" (Eph 6.4). "Fathers, provoke not your children that they be not discouraged" (Col 3.21). A father's loving, carefully thought out training includes reproof and restraint that brings about respect for the parents and reverence for the Lord. His care and wise words encourage children to wise actions, rather than riling them up until they give up.

God gives his children firm and loving discipline; "For whom the Lord loves He chastens… God deals with you as with sons; for what son is there whom a father does not chasten? (Heb 12.6–7 NKJV)

Verse 11 gives purpose to punishment: "Now no chastening seems to be joyful for the present, but painful; nevertheless, afterward it yields the peaceable fruit of righteousness to those who have been trained by it." The Bible does not condone or encourage verbal, psychological, or physical abuse. Scriptural discipline does not create an atmosphere of anger, fear, dread, humiliation, depression, oppression, or injury. It yields "peaceable fruit."

If father leaves the discipline and "can't do's" for mother, showing up only for fishing and sports events, she becomes mama killjoy, and he, pal dad. If mother, with a "Wait 'til your father gets home," saves all problems or punishment for him, the children will dread his homecoming and see him as the bad guy. If dad doesn't back mom up, or she openly looks down on dad, the children take advantage while being disadvantaged. Chaos and insurrection can result. God's plan brings peace and stability to the home.

"Children obey your parents in the Lord; for this is right. Honor your father and mother" (Eph 6.1–3 NKJV). Parents have the responsibility to lovingly teach their children by words and example, that loving the Lord and being respectful and obedient is doing the right thing. This also sets a pattern of respect for other authority figures such as teachers, and those who represent the laws of the land, and lessens needless mistakes and consequences as teenagers and adults. (1 Pet 2.13–17; Rom. 13.7)

Children, being individuals, can complicate this picture. "A wise son heeds his father's instruction, but a scoffer does not listen to rebuke" (Prov 13.1). Proverbs 30.17 warns the one who "mocks his father, and scorns obedience to his mother" (NKJV). Two children can be given the same instructions—one might mock and the other obey. One might ridicule with impudent eyes and manner, or appear to listen but then disobey, and the other shows respect for what you have to say.

As you know, a child's behavior can be affected by things such as mental, physical, and emotional makeup, diet, stress, surroundings, and parental input and example. When there is a troublesome pattern, letting them overhear that "He's the problem child," or "She's stubborn," can encourage the child to claim the behavior and keep acting it out.

Trying to see from a child's viewpoint might change a parent's approach or reaction. During a large store's early morning, people-packed, year-end sale, a small boy was crammed into a table piled high with 50 percent off towels. He began to whimper. Soon his harried mom looked down below table level into his teary eyes in his little flushed face, in a sea of knees, where it had been brushed by rough winter coats, and slapped by slick shopping bags, and loudly scolded: "Stop it! Right now! You are whining—and there's no reason for it!"

Treating your children with loving kindness helps them learn kindness toward others. Teach them to be kind to other children. Meanness and bullying at school can continue right on into adulthood where it continues to devastate lives.

Pro Teen

Young mothers often "dread the teenage years." Many mothers of teenagers "can't wait 'til they're over," and older mothers "barely survived." One challenge is the fine line between being caring, aware parents, or being overprotective. Don't we wish the line were thick—and fluorescent orange? When is a mother "looking well to the ways of…" and when is she using smother love that can cause the teen, like the root bound plant, to try to break the pot in order to grow?

A positive approach helps with many challenges. Nutritionists say growing teens need protein. They also need another kind of nourishment: Pro teen. Pro teen comes packaged as positive input. During this exciting, boring, energetic, tiring, focused, confusing, fun, stressful time of their lives, teens need their parents to love them, encourage their spiritual growth, help them develop their potential, support their positive plans and worthwhile interests, help them rethink their foolish ones, and teach them self-discipline. Dad and mom gradually give them more freedom as their age and level of trust and responsibility determines.

Pro teen doesn't mean they get to get away with disrespect, make their own rules, snore through chores, skip schoolwork, or keep their room in a state of perpetual pig pen, but constantly criticizing everything from hair to homework to posture can affect their inner posture. The challenge is to channel their spirit, not kill it (Prov 15.4).

Choices

The Bible blesses parents and teenagers with wisdom and insight to face their many challenges and temptations. The book of Proverbs provides interesting times for parents and teens as together they seek the wisdom to see situations as they really are; to make choices knowing both the positive, or painful consequences.

For example: To drink or not to drink.

The media portrays the carefree, sure-footed, clear-eyed, good time party guy and girl guzzling and giggling on into the night, or tuxedoed young men and animated young women sipping tall glasses of sparkly liquor in swirly, smiley, serene scenes of sophistication, before their wine-smoothed words change to "urp-slop, bring the mop."

As society continues to glamorize drinking, Proverbs 23 helps think it through by asking "Who...?" Verse 29 begins:

"Who has woe?"
"Who has sorrow?"
"Who has contentions?"
"Who has complaints?"
"Who has wounds without cause?"
"Who has redness of the eyes?"

Six questions. Consider the answers in verse 30: "Those who linger long at the wine, Those who go in search of mixed wine."

Help your teenagers heed the vivid, timeless, advice of verses 31–35. "Do not look on the wine when it is red, when it sparkles in the cup, when it swirls around smoothly; at the last it bites like a serpent, And stings like a viper. Your eyes will see strange things, And your heart will utter perverse things. Yes, you will be like one who lies down in the midst of the sea..."

You'll be on the red-eye special; seeing "strange things." Now it's your seasick head that's swirling, and the sweet stuff you drank to ease your pain, bites and stings. You're angry: "Who's hammering on my head?" You're whining, "When will this nightmare be over so I can 'seek another drink'?"

Instead, seek "wisdom," which is like sweet honey "to your soul" (Prov 24.13–14 NKJV). "For wine is a mocker, strong drink is a brawler, And whoever is led astray by it is not wise" (Prov 20.1). Its effects swirl and spill over for generations; your offspring and theirs will be mopping up your mess.

"Big Bird"

The Proverbs 31.27 woman carefully considers the ways of her household unlike the ostrich (Job 39.13–18).

> The wings of the ostrich wave proudly,
> But are they the pinions and plumage of love?
> For she leaveth her eggs on the earth,
> And warmeth them in the dust,
> And forgetteth that the foot may crush them,
> Or that the wild beast may trample them.
> She dealeth hardly with her young ones;
> as if they were not hers;
> Though her labor be in vain, she is without fear;
> Because God hath deprived her of wisdom,
> Neither has he imparted to her understanding.
> What time she lifteth up herself on high,
> She scorneth the horse and his rider."

The ostrich is the original "Big Bird." The six to nine foot bird can't fly, but its long legs, two-toed feet, and wind-flap wings sustain speed of 30 MPH, with spurts up to 48. The strength and ability of the mother ostrich to run the race is greater than her affection for her offspring, as she seems eager to take off at any time.

She doesn't use her two-inch eyes to watch over the ways of her nest, or her feathered wings to warm and protect her eggs. She can run, kick, and claw, and hangs with a small support group, yet leaves her young in questionable conditions. They lie in a shallow communal nest with only a thin covering of dust to protect them from the foot that could crush or the beast that could trample. Only a few eggs survive. Mama Ostrich is detached; leaving them down in the dirt "as if they were not hers," while she "lifts herself on high." She scorns danger from horse and rider.

As an ostrich runs in circles when it is unsure, sometimes a mother leaves her nest in order to feather it. Has she forgotten possible dangers? Is she restless, or running scared because of financial calamity? Is her fearless eye on secular success? Each mother must develop the wisdom and understanding to assess the needs of her nest; its comfort, security, and vulnerability, so she can strongly encircle it with warmth and protection.

Does all this diligence sound like too much work? "She does not eat the bread of idleness," but rather reaps the rewards we will see in the next, and final chapter.

Questions

1. Where does teaching from a parent or grandparent begin? (Deut 6.4–7; Luke 2.19; 2 Tim 1.5)

2. What are some ways to apply the teaching techniques urged in Deuteronomy 6.4–7 in the home today?

3. How do some in today's society attempt to diminish the father's role in raising children?

4. Where can single mothers in the church look for help in raising their children?

Strength Training

1. It takes strength "to train up a child..." (Prov 22.6). Circumstances such as family size, support system, finances, health and personality of the children, and the spirituality, personality, and health of the parents make parenting more or less complicated. Still, most parents cherish the love, joy, and challenges "the heritage of the Lord" brings (Psa 127.1–5).

2. No parent is perfect. Pray for wisdom and strength even before your babies are born, then continue to pray for them and with them (Jas 1.5–6).

3. As a family, plan regular Bible study time together, appropriate to age. A wide span in your children's ages calls for creativity. (The older can take part in teaching the younger.) Different times for older and younger can also work.

4. The 31 chapters of Proverbs fit nicely with the calendar for a chapter a day Bible reading. Works well for a teen's private study too. (He or she can choose something from the chapter for family discussion). Proverbs addresses daily living, and beyond. Let the

book's own inspired words broadcast its benefits: Proverbs 1.1–6. Read also Psalm 145.10–13.

Not taking advantage of the Word's wisdom, warnings, and ever-accurate forecast when teaching children, is like letting them play peacefully in the waves while the hurricane looms.

Worthy Women
Mary and Elizabeth

The genealogy of Jesus begins in Matthew 1.1 and ends in verse 16 with these 17 soul-shivering words, "And Jacob begat Joseph the husband of Mary, of whom was born Jesus, who is called Christ."

When Joseph, a righteous man, and Mary were engaged, God sent the angel Gabriel to Nazareth of Galilee to Mary, with a startling message. When he had "come in" he greeted her saying "Rejoice, highly favored one, the Lord is with you; blessed are you among women" (Luke 1.28 NKJV). Troubled, Mary tried to understand the angel's joyful pronouncement. He soothed her fears, then further astonished her saying, "And behold you will conceive in your womb and bring forth a son, and shall call his name Jesus. He will be great, and will be called the Son of the Highest" (vv 31–32).

Mary, being a virgin, questioned him. He explained that it would happen through the Holy Spirit, and the power of "the Most High." Next, he surprised and assured her with the news that her elderly relative, Elizabeth, known to be barren, was now carrying a son "in the sixth month." "for with God nothing will be impossible…"

Mary said, "Behold the handmaid of the Lord; be it unto me according to thy word (vv 34–38). Before, we only knew she was young, engaged, probably poor, from a town small enough for everyone to know each other. Now, her "here am I the Lord's handmaid, ready to trust and serve" response reveals her humble heart of faith.

With sober-minded purpose and acute awareness of her great new responsibility, she went "with haste" to the Judean hill country to the home of Elizabeth, whose husband Zacharias was a priest.

They "were both righteous before God, walking in all the commandments, and ordinances of the Lord blameless" (Luke 1.6).

Imagine their meeting: two godly women, one young and one old, each bearing a son, one before she planned, and the other after she thought possible. Each a miraculous event.

As did the worthy woman of Proverbs 31, Elizabeth "opened her mouth with wisdom." Her elderly voice strengthened with excitement and spiritual realization, her tongue spoke words of wonder, kindness, and humility as she blessed Mary and asked "But why is this granted to me, that the mother of my Lord should come to me?"

Then Mary's sweet-strong voice revealed the heart that God had chosen to be the mother of His son. With unusual spiritual depth in such a youthful soul, she rejoiced, praising her Lord and Savior and exulting at the divine blessings He bestowed over her humble status. She praised His might, holiness, mercy, strength, justice, and prophecy, with obvious knowledge of Old Testament teachings (Luke 1.39–55).

Think of the spirituality of these two women. Elizabeth, older in age and spiritual maturity and experience, was six months into her pregnancy with the forerunner of Jesus. The younger Mary was at the edge of experience that would stretch and try her spirit as she carried out the birth of this miraculous conception and mothered the Son of God.

During their three months together they probably chattered excitedly as expectant mothers would; what their babies would look like, when Mary could expect to feel her baby's first kick, and how warmly to dress him. They would also talk about God's extraordinary plan for their sons and the way their lives would intertwine, and would pray for strength and wisdom for their privileged part in them.

Mary returned to Nazareth. Elizabeth, with neighbors and relatives, rejoiced at the birth of her baby. She and Zacharias made known his name, John, and Zacharias prophesied that he would "go before the face of the Lord and make ready his ways" (Luke 1.57–63).

Joseph and Mary went to Bethlehem for the census when she "was great with child." Her time came that "she should be delivered," "And she brought forth her firstborn Son and wrapped him in swaddling clothes, and laid him in a manger, because there was no room for them at the inn."

An angel, joined by a heavenly host praising God brought the "good news" of "great joy" to shepherds living in the fields. They hurried to Bethlehem to find Joseph, Mary, and the baby Jesus, to worship him, and tell what they were told. "Mary kept all these sayings pondering them in her heart" (Luke 2.4–7).

As required by law, Joseph and Mary took Jesus to Jerusalem to "present him to the Lord." In the temple the righteous, devout Simeon held him with great contentment of heart saying he could now depart in peace having seen "thy salvation…" He blessed Joseph and Mary, and then to Mary spoke a sobering, sorrowful prophecy; "Yea, and a sword shall pierce through thine own soul." They returned to Nazareth, "And the child grew, and waxed strong, filled with wisdom; and the grace of God was upon him" (Luke 2.22–39).

On the way home from the annual Feast of the Passover, when Jesus was 12, Joseph and Mary couldn't find him in their group. They returned to Jerusalem and were astonished to find Him in the temple listening, and asking questions of the teachers. When Mary asked why He had concerned them so, Jesus answered, "Knew ye not that I must be in my Father's house?" He went home with them "and his mother kept all these sayings in her heart." She had much to ponder as she observed and experienced his growing years, and also put her thoughtful heart into raising their other children. "And Jesus advanced in wisdom and stature, and in favor with God and man" (Luke 2.42–51).

Mary witnessed His first miracle at a wedding feast in Cana. Later, seeing Jesus hanging on the cross at Golgotha with a crown of thorns on His head, and hearing the cruel crowd mocking Him, a soul saddening scene even to read about, she must have remembered Simeon's words, "Yea, a sword shall pierce through thine own soul." At one time she was close enough to Jesus for Him to entrust her care to "the disciple whom he loved." How joyous must have been the news of His resurrection (John 19.25–27).

Acts 1.12–14 gives our last view of Mary, back in Jerusalem in the upper room with the apostles, other women, and the disciples. The worthy, thoughtful, "Mary the mother of Jesus," now deepened and wisened by the joy and the sorrow experienced as the mother of the Son of God, still filled with the awareness of His great purpose, continues to pray, and live out "Behold the handmaid of the Lord" (Matt 1.16; Luke 2.35, 52; John 19.25–27; Acts 1.12–14).

Facets
Anywhere with Jesus

Deuteronomy 6.4–7 urges parents to teach God's word to their children, and emphasizes the opportunities for heart to heart talking and teaching from "rise up" time to "when you lie down."

Songs can help settle God's word in children's hearts. One day our then young teen grandson said to our daughter, "Mom, I don't know what song to lead for the song leading class." Melisa said, "How about 'Anywhere with Jesus'? It's one of my favorites. We sang it on car trips growing up."

Growing up, I didn't learn Bible related songs since my parents, though good moral people, weren't Christians until in their forties, and we didn't go to church when I was little. Meanwhile, in our two-room school house, our teachers taught us simple songs of then and earlier days. So now, some 60 years later, I'm suddenly singing "She'll be comin' round the mountain when she comes, she'll be comin' round the mountain when she comes..." Now where did that come from? Oh, yes. Mrs. Sloan. Oak Grove Grade School.

What is put into children's minds can pop up at unexpected times, even many years later. So fill your children's hearts and minds with Bible verses and songs "when you rise up," "when you sit in your house," "when you walk by the way," or zoom down the freeway. Then perhaps in later years, when their heart is joyful, or their soul is shaken, they'll find themselves singing "Jesus Loves Me," "Trust and Obey," or "Anywhere With Jesus."

THIRTEEN

Her children rise up and call her blessed;
Her husband also, and he praiseth her, saying
Many daughters have done worthily,
But thou excellest them all.
Grace is deceitful, and beauty is vain;
But a woman that feareth Jehovah, she shall be praised.
Give her of the fruit of her hands;
And let her works praise her in the gates.

I stood squeezing our six-month-old baby boy tightly as our young son and daughter clung to my legs. The popping sound of breaking glass shattered the silence of the night as we watched flames shoot through the front window of the house we finished moving into only an hour before. While we ate a moving day hamburger at a nearby restaurant, a mattress smoldered against a wall heater in the family room.

At last the shrill siren sounds of fire engines announced my husband had rousted a neighbor to phone for help. But, on this snowy December twenty-third, the icy streets slowed the fire engines as our holiday gift wrap quickened the blaze.

Sparks reached the transformer on the pole nearest our house, sending more sparks swirling, creating a clashing, carnival-like effect against the dark sky and snow-covered ground, while shock waves electrified our minds.

Through my smoky, teary, haze of fright, I was acutely aware, and deeply thankful to God that my most precious possessions, my husband and children, were safe outside our burning house.

Later, Al and I spent three cold, depressing days identifying grey, flaky bits of our belongings at the scorched end of the house for a seemingly heartless insurance adjuster. But even then, we were warmed and cheered knowing only material things were in those ashes. When we returned from a friend's funeral to find a "just wanted to help" garbage collector had mistakenly taken the boxes of salvaged items from the carport, near the garbage cans, we still knew they were only material things.

Danger to your family dramatically reminds you of their worth to you. Your love for them makes their love and respect precious. In Proverbs 31.28–29, the worthy woman's family begins to express her worth to them.

Finale of Praise

Verse 28 begins a four verse finale of praise to the worthy woman.

First, "her children rise up, and call her blessed." Their praise goes beyond the "My mommy bakes better cookies than your mommy," of younger children. Young children can learn to "Honor your father and mother," but the praise in this verse probably came from children old enough to realize not only their mother's devotion to them, but to their father, and their heavenly Father.

The love and sacrifice parents think their children take for granted no doubt are, as seen through a child's eyes, just as we aren't capable of comprehending the love, constant care, and blessings received from our heavenly Father. Parents teach children "Please" and "Thank you," but they aren't expected to appreciate the all-out effort that goes into raising them until they become parents themselves. Even then it is an ongoing process. Their parents are often still realizing things about their parents that explain earlier actions and bring new appreciation for them.

For "call her blessed" in verse 28, *Young's Analytical Concordance to the Bible* gives "to pronounce happy." Attitude is obvious to children. The worthy woman's children see her happiness in loving and caring for them. She doesn't feel like an unpaid maid or think of them as a hindrance to her fulfillment. A mother's daily willing attitude helps her daughters look ahead to one day enjoying their nests, and her sons to take an enlightened part in their future nest building.

Reward Snatching

One spring from my bedroom window, I daily watched a robin building her nest, twig by twig, in a sturdy branch of our 100-year-old oak tree, before settling in to hatch her eggs. Then one day, I heard the frightful squawking of a hawk snatching the mother from her nest. When the episode ended all that was left of the once snug little scene were bits of blue shells below and a few feathers clinging to the empty nest above.

Today, it is even more distressing to hear frightful feminist voices urging mothers from their nests. Their hawkish screech contrasts with the robin song of Psalm 127.3: "Behold, children are a heritage from the Lord; The fruit of the womb is his reward" (Psa 139.13–16).

Some in society disdain the "fruit of the womb" and take extreme measures to render it fruitless. Scorning Scripture, they reject His "reward" and promote abortion on demand, even late-term abortion. If they could look into the eyes of our six adopted grandchildren, and countless like them, they would see shining back to them a gleam of the precious rewards and happiness missed.

Her Husband's Praise

In verses 28–29 the worthy woman's husband "praiseth her, saying many daughters have done worthily, but thou excelleth them all."

He uses two forms of the word worth, "worthily" and "excellent," in this one sentence to honor his "far above rubies" wife. His impassioned praise proclaims her lifelong devotion to doing "him good." He trusts his godly wife with all his heart, and she brings him "gain" in every area of their life together.

She is "a crown to her husband." She is not "as rottenness in his bones," making him "ashamed" (Prov 12.4) but contributes to his good reputation "in the gates." While "in the gates" he would learn of other women, "daughters," who had "done worthily," but he tells his worthy woman, "thou excellest them all."

On those "just a housewife" days when your self-esteem sags, and you begin to question your worth, out of the past comes this honorable husband's voice paying tribute to this wife and mother's exceeding worth: "Many daughters have done worthily, but thou excellest them all." You are refreshed as this homemaker receives deserved praise. Many a wilted wife and mother who is doing her best for her husband and children would be revived by a big bouquet of "You're the best."

Through this verse we see mutual commitment receiving rightful reward as he praises his virtuous wife and she thrives on his praise and appreciation. Each husband's personality and needs are different. What one likes, another might not. So it seems the finest praise you can receive from your husband, the person you most want and work to please, is for him to say you are the best wife he could ever have, or, in the words of the worthy woman's husband, "You excel them all" (NKJV).

Is Fluff Enough?

Verse 30 shows the firm foundation for this finale of praise for a worthy woman: "Grace is deceitful, and beauty is vain; But a woman that feareth Jehovah, she shall be praised." This verse first shows who a worthy woman is not, then who she is.

"Grace is deceitful." Grace, or charm, in verse 30 is the ability to please or persuade by the outward appeal of form and manner of expression. These traits can be tricky. Charm and charisma can manipulate a mask of deceit over a cunning character, like the striped tail raccoon that looks so cute and harmless behind its striking black mask. But, if challenged, its little paws reveal claws as it hisses and snarls through its sharp teeth.

"And beauty is vain." Socrates called beauty a "short-lived tyranny." Desire for physical beauty can consume a woman's life, then after its pursuit has taken her time and money, she finds time still takes her beauty.

When the earlier mentioned young model was asked about the feelings she might face when her modeling days were over she said, "You were that pretty thing for awhile and that's what counts." False values are learned young. As early as kindergarten, beauty and name-brand clothing can bring popularity and a superficial sense of importance. Society, aided by the media, moves this thinking right on into old age where some who worry they no longer look young, withdraw from public view or withdraw their life savings to have their falling faces propped up. Self-esteem withers if you don't bloom early enough—or you wilt too soon.

Good stock isn't always packaged in good looks. I learned this lesson early when the soft, curly puppy that cuddled up to my little girl heart was passed over for my older brother's choice of a stocky bundle of rust colored bristles. But the feisty part chow soon proved his worth as he raced ahead of our sun-bared feet, his coarse fur catching threatening thistles, and his sharp bark alerting us to rattlesnakes. When he once surprised a skunk that in turn surprised him, we loved him just the same.

Husbands who choose wives for their outward attributes can feel deceived. Charm and beauty don't guarantee character qualities necessary for a stable and satisfying marriage. Husbands can also capture wives with their charisma and disappoint.

A woman can be deceived by her own charm or beauty. If she merrily manipulates her way through life, she might not end up with the hoped for prestige and peace. If charm and beauty pave a pleasant path for her, assuring advantages when young, she doesn't develop the fortitude that could one day be needed. If life serves up circumstances that require inner oomph—the fluff won't be enough.

Inner Splendor

Society is fascinated with the physical. Outward beauty is common today with the thriving cosmetic industry ever ready to take up where born beauty left off. But what about spiritual beauty? Does inner strength and beauty sound dull? Its pursuit is not only exciting, it replaces pressure with peace. "But, to be spiritually minded is life and peace" (Rom 8.6; cf. 2 Cor 4.16–18).

Many women do have a beautiful physical frame that houses a lovely interior. The same was true of Bible women such as Sarah, "A fair woman to look upon," who is looked upon as a woman of faith in Hebrews 11. Abigail was "of good understanding, and of a beautiful countenance." The "lovely and beautiful" Esther, who "obtained favor in the sight of all who saw her," used both her outer and inner beauty for good (Gen 12.11, Heb. 11.11, 1 Sam. 25.3, Est 2.7, 15, 4, 4.16).

Stand in Awe

The second part of verse 30 identifies a worthy woman as "a woman who fears the Lord" (NKJV). Fear, in this verse, means reverence and awe. Fear of the Lord puts spiritual substance and perspective to the moral and physical facets of her life.

God is the foundation of her multifaceted life. He is the essence of her excellence and strength, the fountainhead of her wisdom and serenity. She works "willingly" as His servant. God is the reason her husband can say "You excel them all."

Today many don't revere God or His word. Some deny Him, and ridicule the Bible, even confidently assume to change it; to subtract from, or add to it, though His word warns, "Do not add to His words, Lest he rebuke you, and you be found a liar" (Prov 30.6 NKJV). "Stand in awe, and sin not" (Psa 4.4).

Stolen Identity?

One afternoon, about age eleven, I stood gaping in wide-eyed fear at a large, leathery rattlesnake. It coiled down in the shaded dirt to my left, its raised head about two feet from where my bare toes met the edge of the wooden step leading into the back of the house. I froze. Then I realized something strange. The rattlesnake wasn't rattling. My three brothers kept a small box of rattles, testifying that rattlesnakes rattle.

Could this be the granddaddy bull snake I stepped on earlier in the strawberry patch at the end of the house? I hesitated, then eased open the heavy homemade door, and ran to my father. His shovel solved the mystery. "It's a rattler all right." As he spoke, my eyes followed his to the blunt, scarred end of the dead snake where buttons had once been before being snagged on a log, rock, or chopped off by an earlier shovel.

Satan, like the rattlesnake, doesn't always rattle a warning; "Hey, I'm Satan, coiled and ready to strike." So, frozen in his influence, you hesitate, mesmerized by the moment, questioning if sin is sin, sometimes staying under his spell until he punctures your life with his poison.

Satan is deceitful; the earliest identity thief: "I fear, lest somehow, as the serpent deceived Eve by his craftiness, so your minds may be corrupted from the simplicity that is in Christ" (2 Cor 11.3). If we lose our fear of the Lord we easily succumb to Satan's deceit, then lose our identity as Christians. "Do not be wise in your own eyes; Fear the Lord and depart from evil" (Prov 3.7 NKJV). "But be thou in the fear of Jehovah all the day long: For surely there is a reward; And thy hope shall not be cut off" (Prov 23.17–18). Run to your Father.

Fruit Bearing

"Say to the righteous that it shall be well with them. For they shall eat the fruit of their doings" (Isa 3.10). Proverbs 31.31, the last verse in this four verse finale of praise to "a worthy woman," shows her eating the fruit of her doings. She is basking in the blessings harvested from her worthy life.

The "fruit of her hands" spans many areas as these action-packed 22 verses of Proverbs 31 show. Though obviously a well-to-do woman, she uses her own hands in many purposeful pursuits, primarily for her husband and children. Her home also provides expansive scope for her talents and abilities, is a ready base of benevolence to others, and creates related interests. Her God fearing wisdom, and the insight and experience gleaned from her lifestyle of "professing godliness through good works" broadens and enriches her abilities and continued activities, increases her inner strength, and produces a peaceful perspective of her life.

Shared Rewards

This worthy wife invested deeply in their husband-wife relationship and now, their love, trust, and commitment, their very oneness, makes it impossible to separate many of the rewards they share. Ecclesiastes 9.9 tells the husband to also enjoy and appreciate his reward in the life he and his wife have together. "Live joyfully with the wife whom you love all the days of your vain life which he has given you… For that is your portion in life, and in the labor which you perform under the sun" (NKJV).

Psalm 128.1–4 presents a family sharing the rewards reaped from walking in "His ways":

> Blessed is every one who fears the Lord, who walks in his ways. When you eat the labor of your hands, you shall be happy, and it shall be well with you. Your wife shall be like a fruitful vine in the very heart of your house. Your children like olive plants all around your table. Behold, thus shall the man be blessed who fears the Lord.

The curtain on this peaceful domestic scene opens and closes with "who fears the Lord." The stage is set with the righteous husband enjoying the fruit of his hands, and the blessings brought by his wife who is devoted to him and his children "in the very heart" of his house. Worldwide, God fearing families still live out this ongoing scene today, bringing joy to all who are privileged to participate or observe.

Mixed Fruit

Simple things sweeten the fruit of each woman's labor, whether living a penny-wise or a plush lifestyle; whether looking out the kitchen window at sunshine on a snowball bush or, in Colorado, out your car window at snowflakes on a buffalo's eyelashes. You taste it in a slice of quiet in a freshened house as a berry pie bubbles in the oven, or in the whole of the love and affection of your family. Both the work of willing hands and heart-tugging tasks bring rewards. For each it's a mixed fruit basket of joy in different varieties, sizes, and seasons.

It can come in the year-round, all-weather, bountiful love of your husband. It can be delighting in the cuddly sweetness of your baby, or the laughing, talking, togetherness times with your children from toddlers to teens. It's savored when their God fearing faith ripens. It's sweetened when your daughter lives the life of a worthy woman, devoted to her husband and children, and as a minister's wife, a teacher of children's Bible classes, and of women in congregations, in jails, and in prison—a servant to others. It smiles through the eyes of your grandchildren, and great-grandchildren. Proverbs 24.3, 4, the inscription chosen by our children and their families for the watches they gave us on our 50th anniversary reads, "Through wisdom a house is built, And by understanding it is established; By knowledge the rooms are filled with all precious and pleasant riches."

Velda

"Let her works praise her in the gates." When a close friend in our congregation was dying from cancer, many praised her saying, "If ever there were an example of a good woman, it's Velda." How had she, in her early fifties, brought such praise? The answer lies in Proverbs 31. Her price was far above rubies. Her husband's heart trusted in her. She worked "willingly" with her hands for home and family, and served others also. She spoke words of "wisdom" and "kindness." She was clothed with "strength and dignity." "Her children rose up and called her blessed." Her husband praised her saying "thou excellest them all."

Still, as with the Proverbs 31 worthy woman, the answer lies deeper, within verse 30. She was "a woman that feared Jehovah," resulting in a life that was praised in the gates. People praised her quiet excellence of character, her whole-hearted devotion to her husband, her careful care and love for her children, her obvious delight in her home, and her many kindnesses to others, all in an aura of faithfulness and respect for God. She had not sought praise. It was a natural by-product of her faith and goodness.

An early morning phone call from her husband told us of her death. As the news spread it brought more praise of her character and life. In her death, as in her life, her heart and hands bore fruit to her family, her friends, and her God. She lived with strength and courage, and she died with strength and courage. As she is praised in the earthly gates, so shall she be rewarded in the heavenly gates.

Full Reward

Praise, or its form, is used three times in these last four verses. Just as the worthy woman is a praiseworthy example of an ideal woman, Ruth provides an example of a real woman of Old Testament times whose works were praised "in the gates." Boaz, a mighty man of wealth, of the family of Elimelech praised her, detailing her worthiness.

> It has been fully reported to me, all that you have done for your mother-in-law since the death of your husband, and how you have left your father and your mother and the land of your birth, and have come to a people whom you did not know before. The Lord repay your work, and a full reward be given you by the Lord God of Israel, under whose wings you have come for refuge. (Ruth 2.11–12 NKJV)

God would recognize Ruth's courageous acts involving faith, family, and daily living for "full reward." Later, Boaz again praised Ruth saying, "All the city of my people doth know that thou art a worthy woman" (Ruth 3.11).

Framed In Faith

Proverbs 31.10–31 is an inspired portrait of "A Worthy Woman," an artist in the art of godly living. It is framed in faith, ready to hang on our hearts. This priceless 22 verse portrait of her life moves us to worship the almighty God, love our families, and stretch willing hearts and hands to bless them, our fellow Christians, neighbors, and others new on our helping horizon.

Thank you for revisiting these verses with me. I pray our time together will strengthen us to live as worthy women, in awe of God, rejoicing in His earthly rewards, attuned to the needs of others, that one day we may joyfully "enter through the gates into the city" (Rev 22.14).

Questions

1. What caused the worthy woman's children to bless her?

2. What made her a praiseworthy wife?

3. Is there any facet of our life our fear of the Lord does not affect?

4. In what ways would her works be praised in the gates?

Strength Training

In private, read again the 22 verses of Proverbs 31.10–31. Think on them. How have they impacted your life? Have they empowered you as a worthy woman? How will they continue to do so?

Worthy Women of Today

It seems a fitting finale to the Honor Roll of Worthy Women of ancient days to honor the countless Worthy Women of Today. Women who "rejoice in the Lord" and bring joy to others. Those who work "in delight" with willing hearts and hands, within their homes and without. In service "known in the gates," and sacrifice known only to the Lord.

To honor godly women who love and honor their husbands, love their children, do what is best for them, and make their homes a blessing to others. Those who lovingly serve with "a cup of cold water," or tell another of the "living water." Those who clean and care for the ill. Listen and teach. Who stir soup and stir up souls. Single women who strengthen their spiritual family with their enthusiasm, time, and talents.

Women who pick through their own patch of pain and sorrow to arrange a bouquet of empathy and encouragement for someone going through a similar circumstance. Older women who continue to teach the younger through their words and lives. Those who pray fervently for others, and are the answer to anothers prayers.

Those who guide, and read to those who cannot see. Those who cannot see, but lead others to the light of the Lord. Those who cannot hear, but use God's word to amplify and share their faith. Those who cannot speak, but whose endurance shouts "The Lord strengthens."

Those who sow seeds of love, learning, and laughter in the hearts of children, and sew pillows of comfort in the hearts of the widows, and the homeless. Those who rescue orphaned children. And those who transform the lives of children they adopt. Women who generously lighten financial burdens. Who hug the hearts of the grieving. Who work with an inner dignity that dignifies unpleasant work.

Women who bring spring to others winters with uplifting notes, cards, phone calls, and e-mails. Those who carry the riches of Christ to the simple cells of jails and prisons. Widows who still serve their master, though now without their soul-mate. Those who lift the hearts and hands of the elders, are ready helpers for the deacons, and encourage the evangelist as he teaches.

Elders' wives who bolster their husbands in his soul-watching work, share him and their home, and serve in ways both known and unknown to others. Deacons' wives who uphold their husbands in his duties and kindly help with needs they become aware of through him.

Preachers' wives who live a God centered life, and keep a loving home atmosphere that strengthens her husband's heart for his work. Who reach to responsibilities in younger years that usually are known to older women. Those who sacrificially stretch their arms and lives across the waters.

Christian women everywhere whose many worthwhile works go unnamed, but not undone; who care not for titles or attention. They care.

Praise "in the gates" to all the worthy women of today who worship the "great God and Saviour Jesus Christ," work to bring glory to His name, and sacrifice self to bring others to His kingdom.

Facets
Extra Mile Attitude
This extraordinary worthy woman's extra mile attitude infused her life, just as this admirable attribute permeates lives today. It

transforms a lukewarm Christian to a "He is our life" disciple. It changes a "just a housewife" into an excellent, purposeful home-maker. It separates the so-so employee from one bound for the success seat. It can change the average student to the outstanding.

The above average approach in a worthy woman's life gives our attitude a positive poke. First, verse 10 puts her price at "far above rubies." Verse 11 shows she is exceedingly trustworthy. Her husband trusts his heart to her. Does verse 12 say she will give doing "him good" a try, and see how it works out? She does him good "all the days of her life."

Does she drag through the day begrudging her efforts for her family and others? Verse 13 answers, she works "willingly," or "in delight." Does verse 14 show her shuffling to the market to purchase mediocre merchandise? "From afar" implies interest and ingenuity. Does she get up and get going "whenever" for "whatever"? Verse 15 says she rises early with purpose and plans for her household. In verse 16 the results of her extra energy and forethought go into a profitable purchase, and her plans for it.

Verse 17 shows she exerts strength to stay strong. In verse 18 she astutely assesses her good gain, and adds to her success by lamplight. She eagerly extends her hands, talent, and intelligence toward her work (v 19). Her extra-mile attitude stretches her arms and alms to the poor and needy in verse 20.

In verse 21 she models a cloak of calmness sewn by knowing she has clothed her household with extra warmth for the winter. Next, in verse 22, with enthusiasm and creativity she pursues the possibilities for personal projects for her home and herself. Verse 23: Her exemplary excellence and discretion in all facets of her life contribute to her husband's reputation "in the gates." Verse 24 shows her action attitude, skill, and dependability aimed at increasing her savings.

The "strength and dignity" of the worthy woman cause her to look to the future full of faith, in verse 25. Out of her worthy heart her mouth speaks wise words, and kindness keeps her tongue: verse 26. Verse 27 teaches that her all-out watchfulness over her household reaps rewards idleness could not: Her children "call here blessed" in verse 28, and in verse 29 her husband praises her extra-mile excellence. Verse 30 shows her walking a joyful, stable, in awe of the Lord life that will bring rewards that choosing a crackly surface of deceit and vanity will not.

Verse 31 shows her godly lifestyle of strength, integrity, love, commitment, faith, and worthwhile works being praised "in the gates" as she continues to live the life of an extraordinary woman.

BIBLIOGRAPHY

Bagster, Samuel, *The Analytical Greek Lexicon*. London: Samuel Bagster and Son Limited. New York: Harper and Brothers.

Clarke, Adam, *Clarke's Commentary*, New York-Nashville, Abingdon: Cokesbury Press.

Encyclopedia Judaica. Jerusalem, Israel: Keter Publishing House Ltd. 1972.

Keil, C.F. and Delitzch F. *Commentary on the Old Testament*. Vol. VI. Grand Rapids: William B. Eerdmans. (reprint) 1978.

Kidner, Derek, *The Proverbs*. London: Tyndale Press. 1964.

Spence, H.D.M. And Exell, Joseph S. *The Pulpit Commentary*. Vol. 9. New York: Funk & Wagnalls Company.

Strong, James. *The Exhaustive Concordance of The Bible*. New York: Eaton & Mains. Cincinnati: Jennings & Graham. 1890.

Tenney, Merrill C. *Pictorial Bible Dictionary*. Grand Rapids: Zondervan. 1963.

Thayer, Henry J. *Greek-English Lexicon of the New Testament*. New York: American Book Co. 1889.

The International Standard Bible Encyclopedia. Wilmington, Delaware: Associated Publishers and Authors. 1915.

Theological Wordbook of the Old Testament. Vol. 1 & 2. Chicago: Moody Press. 1980.

Toy, Crawford H. *A Critical and Exegetical Commentary on the Book of Proverbs.* Edinburgh: T. & T. Clark. 1977.

Vincent, Marvin R. *Word Studies in the New Testament.* Grand Rapids: Eerdmans Publishing Co. 1887.

Wilson, William. *Wilson's Old Testament Word Studies.* Mclean, Va: Macdonald Publishing Co.

For more information about
DeWard Publishing Company and a
full listing of our books, visit our website:

www.deward.com

CPSIA information can be obtained at www.ICGtesting.com
Printed in the USA
LVOW071112050812

292989LV00001B/2/P